VOYAGES WITH THE CELTIC SAINTS

Stories and Wisdom for Travelers in Search of Truth

VOYAGES WITH THE CELTIC SAINTS

Stories and Wisdom for Travelers in Search of Truth

JOHN MATTHEWS

Illustrations by JOE MACHINE | *Foreword by* DAVID SPANGLER

With new translations of magical Celtic poems by
CAITLÍN & JOHN MATTHEWS

REDFeather
MIND | BODY | SPIRIT

Cover and interior design by Brenda McCallum
Type set in Possum/Minion Pro

ISBN: 978-0-7643-6879-0
ePub: 978-1-5073-0557-7
Printed in India

Published by REDFeather Mind, Body, Spirit
An imprint of Schiffer Publishing, Ltd.
4880 Lower Valley Road
Atglen, PA 19310
Phone: (610) 593-1777; Fax: (610) 593-2002
Email: Info@redfeathermbs.com
Web: www.redfeathermbs.com

For our complete selection of fine books on this and related subjects, please visit our website at www.redfeathermbs.com. You may also write for a free catalog.

REDFeather Mind, Body, Spirit's titles are available at special discounts for bulk purchases for sales promotions or premiums. Special editions, including personalized covers, corporate imprints, and excerpts, can be created in large quantities for special needs. For more information, contact the publisher.

We are always looking for people to write books on new and related subjects. If you have an idea for a book, please contact us at proposals@schifferbooks.com.

FSC
www.fsc.org
MIX
Paper | Supporting responsible forestry
FSC® C016779

Go dtuga Dia deoch duit as an tobar nach dtrann
May God give you to drink from the well that never runs dry.
—Traditional Irish Prayer

CONTENTS

To Ari Berk for the germ of the idea,
and to all who make the voyage into vision.

ACKNOWLEDGMENTS

I am indebted to the many scholars of Celtic tradition who have gone before, especially Kuno Meyer and Charles Plummer, whose translations of the lives of the saints provided much of the material from which this book was crafted. A deep debt also to my wife, Caitlín, for her peerless work as a translator, for her keen eye (which sought out my mistakes), and for allowing me to reproduce some of her poetry here. And last, but by no means least, to David Spangler for his wonderful foreword.

J.M.
Oxford, 2023

FOREWORD

BY DAVID SPANGLER

We are fascinated by the extraordinary. Every culture has stories of heroes and heroines who transcend the bounds of normal human capacities and demonstrate abilities and feats that are miraculous and even godlike. In recent modern culture, this tradition has found new life in the various superheroes that dominate the comic book market, not to mention the summer blockbuster movies. Nor can we forget that wizards and magicians, from Gandalf and Dumbledore to Dr. Strange and Yoda, share equal billing in our imaginations. Able to tap into secret forces and energies within the universe, they are every bit as compelling as Ms. Marvel, Superman, Batman, Captain America, Spiderman, and others who populate our new mythologies.

It's not surprising that beings such as this capture our imaginations. Their heroic deeds and fantastic accomplishments and their role as guardians and protectors of the common Good against the forces of darkness and chaos provide exciting tales and perhaps some sense of meaning and comfort in our all-too-turbulent world. Good can triumph over evil. There is hope, at least between the covers of a book or in the darkened environment of the movie theater. Such stories inspire us, as they have for millennia whether told around a campfire or around the glow of a television screen.

Such stories, though, are only a momentary respite in between facing the very real and sometimes dangerous challenges of everyday life in our modern world. Heroes do not swing from the rooftops or fly down from the skies to rescue or help us at the last moment. Wizards do not cast helpful spells or work beneficent magic that saves our day or eases our way. The needs and problems of work and family continue unabated, to be met only by the quotidian abilities that are natural to our ordinary lives.

Perhaps part of our fascination with these stories of men and women with extraordinary powers lies in feeling there's a truth here that we're missing. This truth does not lie in the bite of a radioactive spider that conveys wall-crawling abilities, or in the journey through space from a doomed planet to a world where one has superpowers. It lies in the intuition that the "extraordinary" should be available to everyone, not just to characters of fantasy and fiction. May there not be a feeling that even as we enjoy the exploits of these characters, we are selling ourselves short?

Which brings me to this wondrous book.

I have known John Matthews as a friend and colleague for over forty years. He is a scholar and a man of deep spiritual insight and experience. He has written at least one book for every one of the years I've known him and more. Talk about extraordinary! And of all those books, this one, *Voyages with the Celtic Saints*, is my favorite.

On the surface, it's a marvelous telling of the stories of Celtic saints, and what stories they are! They are filled with wonder, miracles, triumph, and awe. These men and women were the superheroes of their time. In their lives and work, we witness the magic that flows when people, nature, and God are united in love and purpose. These men and women lived ordinary lives entwined with attunement to the Sacred, drawing on sacred wells of power and inspiration.

In other words, these are exciting stories. But unlike the tales of superheroes in our comic books and on the movie and television screens, these stories are real. These individuals walked in the world and met with the ordinary, everyday challenges that all of us meet. And they met those challenges in a spirit of the wholeness of themselves and of the world, a consciousness of attunement to nature and to God.

What makes this book special is that it is more than just wonderful storytelling. John's gifts as a bard are evident throughout in the prose that draws us into the lives of the men and women about whom he is writing. But John offers much more than just stories. He consistently draws back the veil to show us that we should not be confused or put off by the term "saints," or even by overtly religious symbolism, though he is always respectful of the latter. He shows us that what made these men and women remarkable was that they tapped an inner spirit that is innate in each of us. No radioactive spiders here to turn an ordinary person into something special; just joy, compassion, humor, diligence, perseverance, courage, determination, and, above all, a love for people, for nature, and for the sacredness that unites us all into a community of life.

Truly, this book *is* a voyage into Light. It is a journey in the company of fourteen ordinary men and women into the Light that is within the world and within each of us. It is a journey to the sacred wells of inspiration, healing, and love that bubble forth from sacred springs in each of our hearts. They are the wells of our own spirit uniting with the spirit of the world to honor all life, all nature, all the possibilities and potentials that can unfold.

If this sounds too fantastic to believe or too difficult to achieve, then that is a measure of how far we have come in our modern world from a true assessment of who we are. We project our hidden selves, our dormant potentials, onto characters of fantasy and whisper, "If only . . ." What John shows us in this book in the lives of the men and women about whom he writes is that "If only" can become "Of course!" We need to adjust our vision of who we are and of the world we inhabit. We don't need capes or masks or spandex costumes. We just need the sacredness that is the wellspring of who we are. We have kept our identities secret for too long even from ourselves.

With John Matthews as our able bard and guide, it is time to take our voyage into vision.

David Spangler
Issaquah, Washington 2023

INTRODUCTION

VOYAGES OF THE SOUL

Look you out
north-eastwards
over the mighty ocean,
teeming with sea-life;
home of seals,
sporting, splendid,
its tide has discovered fullness.
—J.M. (translation from James Carney)

...

The central theme of this book is voyaging. Voyages of the soul, voyages of the heart, voyages of the mind—voyages. Voyages through the world and beyond the world. Voyages into light, drawn from the lives of the Celtic saints, those remarkable men and women who sought to better understand the world in which they lived, first of all by turning inward and considering the soul's journey, then by turning outward to study the movement of the tides and the circling of the stars, finding there the natural rhythms of life and death reflected.

All of us are engaged on such a journey—however we choose to interpret it. It may be the journey from morning to evening, from birth to death, from war to peace, or it may be the journey that is our search for meaning, truth, or validity. It is this journey that permeates our whole life and that often promotes within us a sense of longing and discontent, whether for the place we came from or the place to which we are headed.

Along the way we will meet others who possess the certainty of their goal, their destination and others who express their passage through life in a wandering fashion, seemingly as directionless as the others are purposeful. We ourselves may fall into either category, or sometimes, into both. There will be periods when we feel confident, directed in our journey. At others we may feel a boundless sense of loss and bewilderment, when the journey seems pointless, directionless, static. It is at times such as this that we turn to others for direction and, if we are fortunate, find it in the person and presence of a friend whose journey is at a different stage, who has passed through the point where we find ourselves, who knows the treacherous shoals or violent undercurrents of the sea on which we both are embarked.

It is just such fellow journeyers as these that constitute the subjects of this book. They are the saints of the Celtic people, men and women who saw divinity in everything and who undertook the journey with a sense of purpose. Natural wisdom was their cauldron, and they drew deep draughts from it. They sought to express the purpose and purity of all life in their own journeys. They had two names for themselves: Celli Dé, "the Children of God," and *peregrini*, "voyagers" or "wanderers," terms that perfectly describe the twin poles of their lives: their belief in the family of the created universe, and their desire to traverse its every part, whether in the spirit or the flesh.

The names of more than 10,000 Celtic saints have survived, some of them recorded only in the land, as place-names that summon up long-forgotten events, legends, and miracles that have vanished, along with their owners, back into the mists from which they came. Aidan, Columba, and Ninian; Bridget, Ciaran, and Kevin; Samthann, Maedoc, and David—their names form a litany, memorials of a past that is long since gone—but that, in our own times, has acquired an urgent energy.

The stories of these people have something to tell us. Something both about ourselves—about our own soul's journey—and about the environment in which we live. They can help us mend some of the broken fragments of the past and the present. From the loam of their examples comes a new growth, a rich heritage upon which we can draw. Their journeys tell us about our own world, about the spiritual voyage on which we have already embarked. Their voices come to us strongly, echoing down the years, relaying their passionate regard for nature, their sense of timelessness, their knowledge of other worlds.

A whole genre of stories—Immrama, literally "rowings about"—treat of these voyages, outlining them in images as clear as the water that bubbles out of the ground at a hundred sacred wellheads scattered throughout the Celtic landscape. Through these we can follow the adventures of St. Brendan "the Navigator," who sought a secret country, and whose voyage took him to a series of islands representing stages on the soul's journey.

Not all the Celtic saints found their way by water. Others loved the land as much or more. Their journeys, still to different states of being, took their qualities from animal, bird, or fish. St. Kevin of Glendaloch was taught by a blackbird and was followed and helped by animals throughout his life. St. Bridget of Kildare, who grew to share the attributes of an ancient Celtic goddess whose name she shared, was the daughter of a milkmaid and took as her symbol the cow whose milk reflected her role as foster mother to Christ. Others took upon them the very nature of the creatures who befriended them: Columba was called "the crane cleric" because of his wisdom; St. Ninian was referred to as "like a bee [who] formed for himself the honeycombs of wisdom"; Patrick expressed his deepest feeling for the natural world in the form of a work that he called "the Deer's Cry." These were not accidental images—the Celtic saints understood the value of keeping in touch with creation through its nonhuman representatives.

Their world was a strange and wonderful place, where fire could be carried in the bare hands without fear of burning, spirits and angels conferred with, wild animals tamed with a word. But the most wonderful and profound mystery that the Celts have to teach us is about our uniquely intimate relationship with the natural world. We all are wonderful beings and we inhabit a remarkable universe, though nowadays we seldom recognize this. By cutting ourselves off from nature, by telling ourselves that we are separate, unique, powerful in our own right, we are doing the equivalent of cutting off our limbs. No one would call themselves whole without hands or feet; yet, we repeatedly sever our contact with the rest of creation, shutting ourselves up in overheated rooms with the ever-present TV screen and the artificiality of a world created in our own image.

The Celts were the opposite of this. They followed a path of complete involvement with the world about them—not only in the physical world, but through their spirituality, which was itself an outward expression of inner things. Through identifying with the natural world, they were able to place their personal experiences in context. We can do the same. The highly sensitized covering of the soul, which can react so strongly when it feels slighted or attacked in any way, reaches a new point of strength when it is no longer placed at the center of everything. Shifting the center to another place, we become new beings and are able to recognize our own inner journey in the context of a larger whole.

The same is true of the Celtic saints whose stories you are about to read, just as it is true of the Druids who went before them. The shift from "pagan" to "Christian" was for the Celts the smallest of steps; no wrenching of the soul from the extreme of one path to the extreme of another. For almost eight hundred years, from the fifth to the twelfth century, the Celtic church did much to keep alive the traditions of the native people, while at the same time promoting the idea of classical learning. The same love of the land, the same honoring of the spirit, the same dance of life, continued unabated despite the change from many gods to one. The essence of the Celtic deities, who were an inevitable expression of the natural world and the holiness of everything, flowed into the container of the new spirituality and changed it from within. Patterns of the inner life, or the place of the human spirit within the universe as a whole, continued as it always had. It was as if two rivers, one flowing out of the east, the other from the west, met and combined and became an even-greater confluence.

When we read, therefore, in the lives of the Celtic saints, we perceive the same fundamental truths that are present in the lives of the gods and heroes of the past: a love of the earth, of the pattern of the seasons, of the magical presence of the animals, of the beauty of the revealed world.

It is this that has given rise to a belief in the existence of a "Celtic church." In a sense, there never was any such thing. At least, not as a separate entity with its own governing body or fixed rule. The eternal verities remained whatsoever the outward changes, the petty squabbles over the dating of Easter and Christmas and the shape of the monastic tonsure. But the journey toward a world of numinous spirituality continued regardless of individual beliefs, the expression of a spiritual unity that gathered strands of wisdom from all over the Celtic world and made of them something like a whole. This spirituality, drawn from the peoples of Ireland, Scotland, Wales, Cornwall, Brittany, and the Isle of Man, possessed a commonality of imagery and belief that far extended beyond the bounds of Christian theology at the time. It was also, as a recent writer has put it,

very much a child of the pagan culture which preceded it, one that valued poetic imagination and artistic creativity, kinship relations and the warmth of the hearth, the wonder of stories and the guidance of dreams. It was a spirituality profoundly affected by the beauty of the landscape, the powerful presence of the sea, and the swift passage at night of the full moon across open skies. (Edward Sellener)

From this marriage came, in time, a high degree of learning and wisdom that gave us the *Book of Kells*, the elaborate and beautiful high crosses that combined both Christian and pagan ideas, and the idea of the hospitality of the heart, which enabled all kinds of people to meet and share their beliefs without fear. The men and women who taught the truths of the new god never completely lost touch with the old deities of wood and water and stone. They reached behind the identity of deity to the heart of matter itself—and in so doing left behind a legacy that speaks as clearly to us today as they did to the people of that long-ago time. This legacy takes the form of a series of messages: that we should acknowledge our place in the universe as a whole; that we should recognize the holiness in all of that creation, not just our own part of it; that we should undertake our journeys in the knowledge that it is part of an ongoing process of completion. These messages are still embedded in the stories you are about to read, and they are as relevant as they ever were—indeed more so since we have cut ourselves off so much from the rest of creation.

From the meeting of pagan and Christian came a spirituality that combined elements from both approaches to life, death, and the otherworld. While the Celtic monks never really strayed from the course of their beliefs, the color of that belief was subtly changed. Elements of the older faith entered their lives, giving a subtle turn to the stories in which they were framed. Thus, while we hear much of St.

Patrick's attacks on paganism in Ireland, we do not often hear of his response to the enthusiastic followers who cut down a grove of sacred trees in order to clear land on which to build a church. Dismayed, Patrick ordered the trees to be left where they had fallen rather than being used as building timbers, and that another site be chosen. He later said that he could conceive of no worse sound than that of an axe striking a tree in Ireland—scarcely the thoughts of someone determined to stamp out the country's older faith.

In the story of St. Ciaran, who became famous for his relationship with representatives of the animal kingdom, we hear that on his first arrival in Ireland, he was granted a vision of a vast tree growing from the center of the land, islanded by a mighty river. Ciaran's spiritual mentor told him that it was a symbol of the enduring quality of his mission, but Ciaran saw it as something deeper. He was moved to found a monastery near a river in the center of Ireland, and Conmacnoise became one of the most important foundations in the Western world, famed for the learning and wisdom of its monks.

In its five hundred years of semiautonomy, the Celtic church promoted the value of women, whom they allowed to celebrate the mysteries openly and equally (much to the dismay of their Roman brethren); it honored the created world as a place of vibrant life and goodness, addressing God as "Lord of the Elements," and angels as "Shining Ones"; and it made the animal kingdom an important expression of its spirituality. As an anonymous ninth-century poem has it:

> To go to Rome—
> Is little profit, endless pain;
> The Master that you seek in Rome
> You find at home, or seek in vain.
> (Translated by Frank O'Connor)

...

These words could be said to stand as a testimony for the majority of the Celtic saints and echo those of St. Samthann, who said that if one could not find God wherever we are, we will not find him at all.

The work of these holy men and women who had been called by a new god can thus be seen to continue that of the visionaries and seers of an older world, seeking silence and solitariness as a means to opening the doors between the realms of flesh and spirit, and of opening themselves to the natural world at an astonishingly deep level. Indeed, as one reads the lives of these ancient holy people, one cannot help seeing that there is a longing for the brighter colors of the past, and a reluctance to let go of the older traditions. The use of poetic and magical names for matters that had far more prosaic terminology in Eastern doctrine forms a living record of the people who wrote and recorded their beliefs for those who came after.

Much of this is summed up in a poem attributed to the seventh-century Irish Saint Manchan, through which we catch a glimpse of the world in which the Celtic saints lived:

Manchan's Prayer

I wish, O Son of the living God,
O ancient eternal King,
For a hidden hut in the wilderness
To be my dwelling.

And, quite near,
A beautiful wood,
Nursing many-voiced birds,
Offering me shelter.

A warm southern aspect,
A little brook crossing the floor,
A choice land with generous gifts
To nurture every plant.

A few good men—
The number does not matter—
Humble men to pray
Daily to the King of Life.
A pleasant church
With a linen altar cloth,
A dwelling-place for God,
A candle to light the scriptures.

This is the husbandry I seek
The bounty I would wish for—
Hens, salmon, trout, and bees,
Food enough for all.

These gifts from the King of Heaven
I would pray for every day,
Seeking to be seen
In the place I had made.
—J.M. after Kuno Meyer

...

These simple requests—for food, a roof, and a quiet place in the woods—epitomize a generation of people who sought to preserve a way of life that was already passing and to inspire those who came to listen to them with the wonder of creation. They taught that the natural world, and the creatures that filled it, were filled with a holy and ineffable light—that same light that drew them to travel to the ends of the earth and beyond into the Otherworld, in search of those visionary truths that all need but few think of seeking for themselves. Their lives are a triumphant expression of wholeness, or inner certainty—qualities that gave them the strength to see their own journeys—seldom easy or comfortable—through to the end.

If there are three essential aspects to the spirituality of the Celtic saints, they would have to include silence and contemplation, the love of nature, and the love of learning. This triad—a form beloved of the Celts—colors all the stories included here. From them we can learn a great deal about the nature of the spiritual heritage of the saints. We, too, can open nature's book, study the patterns of our lives in the silence of the soul's journey, and learn to value knowledge not just for its own sake, but for the way it shapes and forms us. Each story had been chosen to illustrate one aspect or another of the voyages on which we all are engaged, and at the end of each one you will find brief "Meditation Points," designed to lead on from the story you have just read and to help you connect more directly with it.

This is very much in keeping with the original texts from which these stories are drawn. The original "Lives" were written as exemplars, teaching aids that were hardly ever true biographies as we would understand them today. The lives of these remarkable men and women were seen to hold up a mirror to people everywhere, and while today we might find ourselves hard pressed to emulate them as might once have been the case, we can still learn from them. As spiritual biographies they project the story of the human soul and the stories they tell—dramatic, moving, and inspiring by turns—offer a rich fare for the seeker today.

The stories that make up this book are intended to make you think, to ask questions about your inner and outer voyages. They are full of lore both rich and strange, deriving from a people whose imaginative powers have seldom if ever been equaled. Whether you step with Brendan onto the deck of a ship headed for a strange and wondrous country, or follow the wandering life of Ciaran, or enter the visionary world of Maedoc, you will find here echoes of your own search, of the questions that arise in your life and that fuel your ongoing journey. You will also find, following each of the stories, poems from the Celtic tradition that reflect the mystical relationship that existed between the Celli Dé and the world about them. Many of these are newly translated by myself and Caitlín Matthews.

The majority of the stories you will find here derive from ancient sources. It will be noticed that the majority are of Irish origin. This is simply because there is a far higher survival rate of the original documents that tell of the saints. While there were an equally large number of British, Scottish, and Breton saints, in many cases their lives are fragmentary or in various ways unsuitable for a modern audience. The collections of Irish stories, such as those from the fourteenth-century *Book of Lismore* or the later *Vita Sanctorum Hiberniae*, are rich and full of poetry.

There are fewer female than male saints included, simply because there are fewer full-blown life stories that have survived, and therefore very little evidence to draw upon. I have included two new chapters in this revised edition: St. Samthann of Clonbroney and St. Gobnait of Ballyvourney, both of whom include fascinating material.

Once one begins to look at the range of stories, one sees immediately what a huge variety of incidents they contain. While there are overlaps, episodes that turn up in more than one saint's life, there are far more that never repeat themselves. And the richness of the literary tradition is wonderful. Thus, in one story we read how Senan battles with the Druids, while in the life of David of Wales there is a dark story of murder and sacrifice balanced by a tale of the saint's wondrous horse, which could gallop across the water as though it were on dry land.

In the stories included here, I have sought to find wonder, the expression of spiritual truth, and poetry. In the process, while never purposefully steering the content away from the original intent, I have tried to go to a place where all spiritual paths meet and reflect each other. Thus, I have modified the sometimes extreme monasticism of the writers (who were, after all, monks, as well as fine storytellers) and have chosen to retell those episodes that reflect a larger picture. In this way I hope to make the stories accessible to a wider audience, to set them free of the confines of theology. To this end, I have allowed myself freedom to reshape the original stories, while remaining faithful both to the spirit and occasionally the words in which they were first recorded. This approach not only opens up the stories of the Celtic saints but also shows how much they were indebted to the pre-Christian storytellers, whose works they clearly knew. These stories were always intended to teach by example, and in these current retellings I have tried to allow their innate spiritual messages to emerge into the light of day, where they can be enjoyed by an audience today.

These stories (often written by those who knew the saints personally) celebrate the voyages into vision that these remarkable men and women undertook. At a time when we all are in search of new truths, new ways of looking at old truths, they have much to teach us. They can become our soul friends—*anam chara*—on our own journey, and read with an open heart—just as they were set down with an open heart—they offer a series of beacons to be followed and experienced for ourselves, whatever course our own journey may have taken. The realizations that follow can release a tide of love within us: love for each other and for the world in which we live and move and have our being. As we acknowledge the power of the voyage, and of our own place within it, we awaken as if from a long illness. The blood courses in our veins with renewed vigor, and we turn again to the tasks of daily living with new strength and purpose.

I am especially delighted to see a new edition of this book, which was originally published in 1998 and is now graced with the extraordinary images by Joe Machine, which bring these ancient characters to life in a powerful way. I have taken the opportunity of adding two new chapters, adding two further female saints to the roster, and to making some small corrections to the original text. This version also represents a more accurate version of the text as I wrote it and before editing by the publishers of the time. I hope it may serve, in a very different age to its initial appearance, to bring together the pagan and Christian foundations upon which these stories were founded. And if you want to celebrate their memories and what they stand for, do so on their feast days, all of which are included at the head of each chapter.

John Matthews
Oxford, 2023

ONE

IN SEARCH OF A SECRET COUNTRY

BRENDAN OF CLONFERT
(May 16)

Seven years in all were they
On the voyage—fair was the band—
Seeking the Land of Promise
With its flocks, a strong subtle turn.

And they found it at last
In the high meads of the ocean,
An island rich, everlasting, undivided,
Abounding in salmon, fair and beauteous.
(Navigatio Brendani)

...

With the story of Brendan, we are plunged into a world where the Voyage leads out of this world. Out of ordinary, everyday consciousness, into another place. The Land of Promise it is called here, a name also applied to the Otherworld by pre-Christian Celts. It is the first sign that we are entering a place where two ways meet: the old magic of the Time Before and the new magic of Palestine are joining hands. When Brendan sees an angel who instructs him to set forth on a voyage of inner discovery, he stands in the shoes of older heroes, like Bran mac Febal, who undertook an earlier voyage after a faery woman came to draw him away. In both cases the purpose is the same: angel and faery each comes to offer an opportunity to discover something new and wonderful. Indeed the parallels between the Christian "Voyage of Brendan" and the pagan "Voyage of Bran" are so close as to include the name of certain islands and virtually identical adventures taking place on them. From this we can see that the later storytellers not only knew the older tales but were influenced by them when it came to the description of the otherworldly islands visited by Brendan.

Brendan lived from around 486 to 578 CE. In that time, Christianity had been established in Ireland for some time (St. Patrick—389–461—was its main source), so that Brendan was part of a tradition that had taken hold and was putting down deep roots. Born at Annagh on the bay of Tralee, he became a monk and later an abbot and founded monasteries at Clonfert and Ardfert. He traveled widely, including to Iona, where he met with Columba, as well as to Wales, Britain, and Gaul.

There are over one hundred manuscript versions of the Voyage of Brendan, many of them differing markedly and adding other islands. I have worked primarily from the version ascribed to a "poor friar" named Michael O'Clery and dated 1629. Though late, this version seems to me to capture the wonder and innocence of the story, which so clearly harks back to the adventurers of earlier voyagers in Celtic tradition.

The day that Brendan was born, the whole sky above his village of Alltraighe Caille lit up with fire. The wise bishop Erc said that a great soul had come into the world that night. Brendan was the son of Findlug, who, the night before his birth, dreamed that her breast became golden, as though filled with light. When he heard this, Bishop Erc said that the child was to have a special destiny, and when he was one year old placed him in the care of a woman named Ita. Wise and full of wit, she cared for the child until he was five, at which time the bishop himself took Brendan in and taught him the ways of Christ. Thus Brendan grew in stature and knowledge until he was a young man, when he saw an angel standing in a field of corn. The angel pointed westward, and though he did not understand it then, Brendan ever after wished to go to the west.

Barinthus's Story

One day when Brendan was at a place called Leim na Subaltaige, a man named Barinthus came to see him. Now this Barinthus was known to possess a great knowledge of the tides and the stars and was a great sailor. He told Brendan a story, and this was the way of it.

Barinthus had a son named Mernoc, who, when he came of age, decided to leave home in search of adventure. He was gone for a long while before his father received news of him. He had, it seemed, found his way to an island where there were a number of *peregrini*, holy men who sought to learn the ways of God more deeply through wandering and living in isolation. Desiring to know more, Barinthus set sail and in three days arrived at the island. The peregrini came out of their huts like a swarm of bees, clustering around the visitors as though there were pure honey. Barinthus spent some time with Mernoc and his brethren, learning their ways. They lived simply on the island, eating only apples and nuts, studying the paths of the stars and the movement of the tides, which sang to them day and night.

Then Mernoc came to his father and led him to the shore, where a little boat lay at rest. "Father," he said, "let us get into the boat. It will take us to a place that is called the Land of the Saints, where there are many wonders."

Together they stepped into the boat, which at once drew away from the shore, though no one could see how it was driven or who steered it. A mist settled over the water, so that neither Barinthus nor Mernoc could see where they were headed, until suddenly there was a great light ahead, and the mist began to clear. They found themselves closer to the shore of a new land, where white sands edged the water, and the trees that grew there were heavy with fruit.

Father and son went ashore on this beautiful country, and for the next fifteen days they wandered without seeing anyone. Then they came to a wide river, which blocked their path. On the far bank they could see a place that seemed to them even more wonderful than that in which they stood, but there was no way to cross the river, which ran swift and high between its banks.

As they stood, there came in sight a man who was clad in garments of radiant light. He approached them directly and addressed them by their names. "Beloved friends," he said, "you may not pass beyond the river. This much has been revealed to you so that you may know of its existence and tell everyone you meet of its beauty. For this is the Land of Promise and the Land of the Saints."

Then they asked the man from whence he came and what his name might be. And he answered them thus: "Why do you ask me this? You would be better employed asking about this place. Though you do not realize it, a year has passed since you stepped ashore; in all that time you have never seen the sun set nor wanted for food and drink. This might be the lot of everyone if only they remembered this place. For all have been here, and yet they have lost the way back to it."

Barinthus and his son were saddened by this and turned away. They returned to the boat, and the man accompanied them all the way, talking to them of the ways of the world and the ways of the spirit and how these might be brought together. But when they were arrived at the shore, he vanished away—they knew not how or where. Then they climbed into the boat, which drew away from the shore and sped back across the mist-draped water to the island where Mernoc lived.

The holy men came to meet them and inquired of their journey. Barinthus and his son told them everything that had occurred and said, "You are fortunate indeed, for you live close to the Land of Promise." Then Barinthus took leave of his son and set forth wandering through the world, so that he might tell everyone he met about the wonderful land.

The Voyage Begins

When he had heard this story, Brendan could not rest until he had visited the Land of Promise for himself. For now, he understood the meaning of the angel that had pointed to the west. And that night, as he slept, he saw the angel again, and it said to him, "Arise Brendan. That which you have longed for shall be yours." And the angel told him to choose companions and prepare a ship in which to begin a great voyage.

When he awoke, Brendan did as the angel had bidden. He gathered about him fourteen other men from Leim na Subaltaige and told them that he desired to set forth in search of the wonderful land. And he told them also of the angel's words, and when they heard this they declared that they wished to go more than anything else in the world.

So Brendan and his companions went to a place that ever after was known as Suide Brenainn, Brendan's Seat, from where they looked out upon the ocean. For Brendan knew that it was from here they would set forth. So they set about preparing a small craft and provisioning it for several weeks at sea—for though they had no idea of the distance they must sail, Brendan's inner voice told him that they would find further sustenance when they needed it.

When all was prepared, the company embarked, but just as they were about to set sail, a man clad like a Fool came hurrying up and begged to be allowed to go with them. And, since there was one last place on ship, Brendan gave it to him.

Then they set sail forthwith to the west.

The Island of Hospitality

For days they sailed toward the summer solstice. The wind blew strongly and they had no need of navigation. But after fifteen days, the wind dropped and they were forced to row onward. After a time they grew weary and looked to Brendan for advice. He said, "Do not fear. God's angel is steering us. Ship all the oars and the rudder but leave the sail set. If we give ourselves up to the will of the sea, we shall come to no harm."

They did as Brendan told them, and for the next forty days the craft was driven by fitful winds and wild water. Soon all their food and most of their water was gone. Then they espied an island. To their dismay, it was a high and rocky place with no sign of a safe harbor.

To add to their discomfort, they could see several places where freshwater streams fell over the edge of the cliffs and down to the sea.

At first they tried to sail close to the cliffs and to lean out over the side with drinking vessels in which to catch some of the water. But when he saw this, Brendan ordered them to stop. "We must trust to God's angel to guide us to the right place. In three days, we shall find a landing place. Until then we must bide out time."

Sure enough, on the third day they found an opening in the cliffs, and though it was very sheer and narrow, they managed to steer a course within and found themselves in a sheltered bay. There they disembarked, and there, as they stood upon the land, a dog came and laid its head on Brendan's feet.

"Is this not a good messenger?" said Brendan. "Let us follow it."

In a short time they arrived at the gates of a town, which were open in welcome. Yet, there was not a single person to be seen, and they grew afraid at this. But Brendan encouraged them to enter, and in a short while they saw before them a great hall, with its doors standing open, and inside they found tables laid with bread and wine and fish for all.

Brendan said, "Let us eat, for this feast is sent to reward our endeavor. Afterward you will find beds made ready for you."

So they ate hungrily, and never did food taste better. Then they retired to rest.

For three days and three nights, they rested and were served with such hospitality as they had never known, all without sight of those who served them. Then on the fourth day, Brendan declared that they must set forth again. "Be careful," he said to them, "that no one takes anything from this island—not even water or bread."

And, because of the faith they had in Brendan, they set sail again from the island, without taking any provisions. But before they had gone far, the sails fell limp and the sea was becalmed. Brendan called to all the men who were on the ship. "One of you has taken something from the island. We can go no farther until it is given back."

The man dressed like a Fool, who had come late to the voyage, fell at Brendan's feet and drew from within the bosom of his clothing a bridle inlaid with silver. He flung it down and burst out weeping.

"Let us return to the island," said Brendan.

At once the sails filled and the boat returned by way of the narrow channel to the inlet. There Brendan commanded the one who had stolen the bridle to go ashore and to return it whence it came.

As they were returning to the ship, a youth came toward them along the shore, carrying a basket of bread and a flask of water. "I bring this gift to you, Brendan, with the thanks and blessings of your hosts. You still have far to go on your journey, but neither bread nor water will you lack until you are at your journey's end."

And with this, the company returned to their craft and their voyage continued, and no matter how much they ate or drank of the bread and water, they never lacked for either until they arrived at their next landfall.

The Island of Birds

A few days after this, they sighted another island. Low lying and supporting neither grass nor sand, it seemed an inhospitable place. But the companions were glad to go ashore even in that barren spot and at once set about lighting a cooking fire. Brendan, however, stood on the deck of the ship and watched them with a smile, for his angel had told him the true nature of the island.

In a while, as the fire grew hotter, the whole island began to shake and shiver as if it were about to sink beneath the weaves. The companions grew fearful and hastened back to the boat, where Brendan helped them aboard quickly. Then they pulled up their anchor and watched as the island began to move away from them of its own accord! The companions turned to Brendan for understanding, and he laughed aloud. "Do you not know the nature of this island?" he asked. They shook their heads. "It is no island at all," said Brendan, "but a great fish—the greatest that ever sailed the seas. God's angel has told me that its name is Jasconius and that it sails forever in search of a mate."

The companions marveled greatly at this and watched as their fire vanished into the dusk of the day, carried on the back of the great creature. Then many gave thanks for the wonders that filled the world, and they sailed on, looking always for the next landfall, which might be the gateway to the Land of Promise.

Soon they sighted another island and, drawing up to its shore, dropped anchor there. It was a fair-seeming place, where the grass was starred with flowers in profusion, and a grove of trees clustered on the horizon. Brendan led his companions ashore, and they found a stream of very pure water from which they gratefully drank. Then they followed the course of the stream inland until they reached its source. There a most beautiful tree grew down over the water. Its height and size were remarkable in themselves, but the most astonishing thing about the tree was that it was covered with white birds. So thickly did they cluster on its branches that one could scarcely see its leaves.

Gazing upon this sight, Brendan's eyes filled with tears, and he wept aloud, calling upon God's angel to tell him the meaning of this wonder. As he did so, one of the birds flew down and perched on the side of the boat. The motion of its wings made a sound like the pealing of tiny bells.

Brendan looked at the bird and said, "If you are a messenger, speak and tell me why so many of your kind are gathered here."

At once the bird replied: "We are survivors of an ancient battle between the angels of light and dark. Because we took sides with neither one nor the other, we must remain in the world, able to travel only in spirit form. Only on Holy days are we permitted to take on the shape that you see. For today is Easter, and you have been upon your voyage for a year. Six more years lie before you, but in the end you shall find the Land of Promise."

The companions listened in astonishment to this, for to them it had seemed as though only a few weeks had passed. But Brendan smiled and gave thanks to the bird for its wisdom and watched as it rejoined its fellows. Then the whole company set about preparing to celebrate the Holy festival, setting up a makeshift altar on a flat stone in the shadow of the great tree.

When the time came to sing praises to God for the wonder of creation and the blessing of Christ, the companions gathered about the foot of the tree, and there the birds who sat upon the branches like blossom began to sing, and it seemed to them all that their voices formed words and that they sang as sweetly as a heavenly choir of angels.

And when they had finished celebrating, they prepared to continue their journey. But as they were about to raise the anchor, one of the white birds came again and settled upon the prow of the boat. Once again Brendan said that if this were God's messenger, it should speak, and once again the bird obeyed. "In a year's time you shall return here and celebrate Easter just as you did this day, and you shall meet again with the great creature Jasconius. Sail on now, Brendan, and in time you shall find yourself on an island where only the wisest elders are to be found. There you shall celebrate Christmas."

Having delivered itself of these words, the bird flew back to its place. As the ship drew away from the island shore, they all heard voices raised once again in sacred song.

The Island of Ageless Elders

Now the ship carrying Brendan and his companions sailed for several weeks without sight of land. At the end of this time they saw a new island rising from the sea. But though they made directly for it, they could not, at first, find anywhere to land. For another five days they sailed about, and it was only as they began to wonder whether they might ever find a harbor on this island that there appeared an entrance between high rocks. There they put in to the shore and, stepping out of the boat, found two wells sited close to each other. One gave forth water of such purity that it seemed to shine with its own light; the other was muddy and dark.

At first the companions would have rushed forward to drink, but Brendan stopped them. "I believe we are not meant to drink from either of these wells until we are given permission by those who live upon this isle."

As he spoke, there came toward them a man of great age and gravity. He bowed to them in silence and beckoned them to follow. They made their way through a grove of trees, and there before them was an enclosure with walls of stone. Within it were a number of round huts, clustered around a larger building in the center.

"What is this place?" asked Brendan. "Who lives here?"

The elder did not answer but beckoned them to enter the enclosure. Brendan and his companions looked about and saw a number of men coming from the huts and making their way to the larger building, which, they now saw, was a church, built of timbers and roofed in straw that shone as though made of gold.

Still in silence, the companions were conducted into a refractory, where tables were laid with loaves of extraordinary whiteness. As soon as they were seated, a man came forward with a jug of water and served them all. Only now did the elder speak: "Welcome, voyagers to the Land of Promise! Drink deeply of this water, which will enrich you, and eat of the food we have provided. But do not speak until all have eaten and we have celebrated the bounty of God together."

Thus in silence the travelers and their hosts ate and drank. Never did bread and water taste so sweet. And when they were done, the elder led them to the church. In its cool interior, Brendan and his companions looked around and saw that the building was square and had two altars, each one made of crystal, with vessels of the same wondrous material. Twenty-four seats were set out in a circle around the church, and here the companions were given places.

All was done in strict silence, and they noticed that if any one of the island community wished to convey something to the elder, he went and knelt before the venerable man and spoke not with words but with glances. The elder would listen with his inner senses and write whatever revelation he received on a wax tablet, which he then gave to the one who sought an answer.

Only when silent prayers had been offered up, and the mysteries celebrated with the vessels of crystal, did the elder finally give permission to speak. To Brendan and his companions, he said, " I know you have many questions. Let me answer some of them even though you have not given them voice. We are a community who have lived together here on this island for more than eighty years. In that time, none of us have grown any older or suffered a day of sickness. Every day we are brought sufficient loaves and roots to eat, though we have no idea whence they come. You have seen our two wells. They are a wonder, for one gives the purest water that we ever saw, and the other is constantly warm, so that we may wash ourselves daily and are constantly cleansed and refreshed. Thus we live here in silence for the most part, listening only to the inner voice of God that speaks to us every day and conveys to us the wisdom and spiritual goodness for which all yearn."

"Father," said Brendan, "may we stay here with you? Surely I know of no more wonderful place, unless it is the Land of Promise itself."

"You may not," replied the elder gently. "Nor should you need to ask this, for your road leads elsewhere. I tell you that soon you shall come to another place, the Island of the Three Choirs, and there one of your number will remain, but for the rest you shall journey onward, as it is given you to do."

While they spoke thus, the darkness began to fall, but as the shadows lengthened within the church, a fiery arrow entered through a window and sped through the room, lighting all the lamps that hung before the two crystal altars. Then it flew out again and vanished, none might say where.

"What does this mean?" asked Brendan.

"It is one of the mysteries of this place," replied the elder. "Observe how the light can be seen burning in the center of each bowl. Yet, I tell you that it is never be consumed. In the morning the light will flicker out, and tomorrow it will be lit again just as you saw it now. In all our time here, we have never had to replenish it once. Truly it is a spiritual light."

That night, Brendan and the elder kept vigil together, and in the morning the voyagers were invited to remain on the island until Epiphany, and to celebrate the feast of Christmas there, just as had been foretold.

The Island of the Well of Sleep

When the feast days were over, Brendan and his companions prepared to depart. They provisioned their boat and received the blessing of the ageless elders before raising the anchor and setting forth again. Winds and tides took them, and they sailed on for many days before they sighted land again. This time the island where they landed seemed hospitable.

The companions were eager to go ashore and replenish their stocks of food and water, and when they had disembarked, they found a well of clear water close to the shore. Around it grew plants of many kinds, many of them edible, while in a stream that ran nearby they found plentiful fish.

Brendan told them to gather as much food as they wished, but to be careful about how much water they drank. "For," said he, "it has been made plain to me that we should drink only sparingly of this spring."

Some of the companions chose to interpret this as taking no more than one cup; others thought they should have two; others three. Those who took the most fell asleep almost at once and remained unconscious for three days. Those who two took two cups slept for two days. Those who took only one cup slept for a day and a night and awoke refreshed.

"It seems to me that we should leave this place," said Brendan. And when they had replenished their stocks of food and water, they departed hurriedly, sailing north, though they knew not where they were bound.

The Island of Birds Again

Their course took them again to the Island of Birds, and just as had been foretold, they cerebrated Easter there once again. And before that they found themselves crossing the path of Jasconius, the great creature of the sea on whose back they had camped a year before. But always Brendan drove them onward, longing ever more deeply to see the Land of Promise.

One day when they were far from land, they sighted a huge and terrible beast in the distance, which, when it saw them, turned in their direction. The companions cried out in fear and began to pray aloud to God. But Brendan rebuked them for their lack of faith and commanded them to look again. When they did so, they saw another monster, which breathed both fire and smoke, rise from the water between them and the advancing creature. Then they watched a great battle between the two, and when it was over there were only pieces of the first monster floating in the sea.

Soon after, they saw the shore of a large island covered with trees, and there they landed, glad of the chance to rest and refresh themselves. There, floating in the water of the bay where they had landed, they saw a part of the great beast that they had feared would kill them. Brendan ordered them to drag it ashore and to light a fire and cook it. "For," he said, "that which would have eaten of our flesh, we shall eat instead."

That night they dined well, for the flesh of the beast was particularly sweet, and next morning they set forth again.

The Island of the Three Choirs

Soon after this they espied a new island, very flat and treeless. Brendan looked toward it with his inner sight and said, "On that island are three choirs, just as we were told by the Ageless Elder. One consists of boys, one of youths, and a third of elders. One of us will not return from there."

The companions looked at one another in wonder, for they knew that Brendan was seldom mistaken in his visioning. For as time passed, he was increasingly aware of how things must be, and of the meaning of events that took place on the voyage.

Soon they came to the shore and disembarked. The island was so flat and bare that they saw the three choirs at once. The boys were clad in white robes, the youths in blue, and the elders in purple. All three choirs went about constantly, moving from place to place on the island; only when they sang did they remain still. And since one or other was constantly singing and giving forth praises, the choirs were in perpetual motion, following some rhythm of heart or soul that neither Brendan nor his fellows could perceive. Yet, their song was more wondrous and moving than anything they had heard.

As the day advanced, a cloud of extraordinary brightness settled over the island, so that they could only hear the voices of the choirs but see nothing of them. Thus night fell, and the voyagers slept to the sound of singing. And in the morning they awoke to the same bright song. Then one of the leaders of the choirs came forward with a basket of purple fruit and laid it in the boat. "Now give to us that one among you who has the finest voice, for one of our number has but lately died, and another is needed."

Brendan turned to the man dressed like a Fool, who had been the last to join the company and had stolen the silver bridle. The man stepped forward with tears in his eyes. "I have long known that this would be my path," he said, "and the song calls out to me."

Then they set sail again and were soon far from the island. Yet, still they could hear the songs of the three choirs and marveled greatly at the beauty of their singing. Then they feasted on the purple fruit, which tasted like the finest honey and gave enough juice to feed them all.

The Island of the Crystal Pillar

And so they sailed on for many more days, until they came to a place where the sea was so clear that they could see right to the bottom, and there were numerous hosts of fish swimming in such a way that it seemed to the companions that they followed a pattern. Some were afraid because of this and called to the others to keep silent lest they attract the attention of these strange fish. But Brendan told them to put aside their fear, and he began to sing aloud, encouraging his companions to do the same. Soon they all were singing together, and as they did so the fish began to rise to the surface until they surrounded the boat in their thousands.

There they stayed for many hours, always keeping the same distance between themselves and the boat, flowing around the craft in wide arcs, flashing fins and tails at the voyagers as though in silent salute. Then, just as suddenly, they were gone, and the sea was still.

Next morning the companions espied a pillar rising from the sea. At first it seemed close, but as day followed day and it seemed no nearer, they began to see how vast it was. Four days later they were close enough to see that the pillar stretched so far up into the heavens it seemed to touch the sky itself. Hanging from the pillar was a great net, the meshes of which were so wide that four men could have walked through them without touching. The company was greatly desirous of passing within the net, so that they might examine the nature of the pillar; yet, the net was too small to allow the ship to go through. Therefore Brendan ordered his companions to ship their oars and to unstep the mast. When this was done, they were able to steer between the meshes of the great web and so found themselves close to the pillar.

None could be certain from what substance it was made, though it seemed like crystal. As they sailed around it, they saw that it had four sides, and that each one was carved with intricate patterns, and that here and there, windows and ledges were cut into them. Some spoke of climbing it, but that Brendan forbade, for his angel told him it was not appropriate for them to do so.

That night they anchored close to the pillar, and for several hours after the sun had set they could still feel the heat coming from the pillar. In the morning they sailed on and found themselves on another side of the pillar. There, set in one of the carved niches, they found a crystal chalice, and at Brendan's bidding they took it aboard and used it to celebrate the mystery of the Eucharist.

Then they set forth again, passing once more through the meshes of the giant net. Then, having set the sail and unshipped the oars, they proceeded once again toward the north—for in this direction it now seemed to Brendan they must continue until they reached their goal.

The Island of Smiths

Not long after this, they saw a dark and craggy island on the horizon. Smoke arose from it as though from a hundred fires, and it was bare of all trees or grass.

Brendan frowned. "I do not like this place," he said. "Yet, the wind is driving us closer to it."

As he spoke, they came within clear sight of the island and saw that it seemed the most desolate place they had ever known. Huge piles of slag lay about everywhere, and there were signs that mining and smelting had taken place there for long ages. As the boat drifted nearer, they saw that the island was covered in forges, from which huge, distorted plumes of smoke arose, darkening the sky. As they looked, one of the smiths came out and stared at them. He was huge and hairy, with skin darkened by his work. When he saw the voyagers, he let out a great roar and disappeared into his forge, emerging moments after with a red-hot boulder that he flung high into the air. It passed very close to the boat and fell into the sea, which at once began to boil and bubble.

Brendan ordered the oars to be run out, and they drew swiftly away from the island. More of the shaggy smiths came in sight, each carrying hot stones that they flung toward the ship. It seemed as though the whole island were ablaze with one great fire, and the sea on all sides boiled like a cooking pot. But despite being in mortal fear, the companions rowed steadily, and gradually the island of smiths fell away behind them, until it was only a red stain on the water.

The Island of the Hermit

The next island they came upon was small and desolate. It was hard indeed to find a place to land, and when they had finally done so, Brendan commanded all of them to remain on the boat until he had sought permission from the inhabitants of the island for them to come ashore.

Walking inland, he came to a cliff where the mouth of a cave gaped in the rock. In front of it a small spring bubbled forth, and in front of the spring sat a man whose white hair grew so plentifully that it completely covered him. Other than this he was naked, and Brendan marveled at his fortitude and his serenity.

When he saw Brendan approaching, the aged man rose to his feet and gave a warm greeting, inviting Brendan to bring all of his companions ashore. He greeted them all by name, astonishing them with the power of his inner sight. Brendan praised him and asked him to speak to them of his life.

"My name is Paul," said the old hermit. "Once I was a monk, whose task was to look after the burial place of all the brothers. One day I was preparing a new plot for one who was expected to die soon, when there came to me a stranger who commanded me to dig another grave. When I asked his name, he told me that he was the father of my own monastery, no less than the blessed Patrick himself. He told me that he had died the day before, and that soon they would bring his body to be buried there. Then he swore me to silence and told me to go to the shore, where I would find a boat waiting to take me to the place I needed to be.

"In the morning I did just as the blessed Patrick told me, and there, sure enough, was a little boat with a single sail awaiting me. As I stepped in, the sail filled and it bore me across the ocean to this island. Once I stepped ashore the boat turned about of its own accord and returned the way it had come. Since then I have lived here alone save for a wonderful creature, an otter, who brings me a fish in its mouth every day and has done so for the last thirty years. I live simply in this cave and drink from the pure water of the spring that you see. God takes care of all my needs. I am ninety years of age," the hermit added proudly, "and now I only await the time of my death."

Brendan and his companions listened to this tale in wonder. When the hermit had finished speaking, Brendan asked if they might replenish their water from the spring, and to this the old man agreed. "Be sure," he said, "that you will soon find your way to the Land of Promise, and that it shall be filled with all the wonders you desire."

The Land of Promise

This time their course took them east, and a few days later they encountered the great creature Jasconius. This time it seemed to act as a guide and lead them straight to the shores of the Island of Birds. Thus for the third and last time they saw the great tree and heard the delightful singing of the birds. And there, once again, came one of the birds, who had spoken to them twice before. It welcomed them and said, "You must prepare now for the final part of your voyage. This time I shall come with you, for you will not find your way to the Land of Promise without me. You have proved yourselves well in the time you have been upon this path, and now you shall have your reward."

The bird instructed them to take on provisions for forty days, and in the morning they set sail, the bird standing on the prow of the boat and guiding them.

Forty days exactly after leaving the Island of Birds, they entered a thick mist.

"This mist surrounds the place you have been seeking," said the bird. "You must pass through it to find safe harbor."

The mist was like a curtain, but after a time it lifted and the voyagers found themselves looking at a wide land clad thickly with trees on which the fruit hung heavy. It seemed like perpetual summer in that place, and Brendan and his companions hastened to go ashore and soon as they might. The bird remained behind upon the boat, saying that it was not yet time for it to go there.

So at last Brendan and his followers came to the Land of Promise, and they fell to weeping and embraced each other as old friends will who have shared so much together. What they found in that land can scarcely be set down in words. Food of the spirit and joy in abundance were theirs, and a sense of fulfillment. For in that place was health without sickness, pleasure without contention, union without quarrel, attendance of angels, feasting without end, meadows sweet with the scent of fair blessed flowers.

And indeed, it was all just as the mariner Barinthus had told them. Like him, the companions wandered through a land of radiant light until they found themselves facing a great river, too wide to cross. There, as they stood upon the bank, came a youth who seemed covered with white down as a bird might be.

"Welcome," he said. "You have proved yourselves true to your intent and to the search for truth that led you to undertake this voyage. It is not yet time to cross this river, but you shall return one day, and the way shall be open to you. For now, you may take of the fruit of this land, and any other riches you may find. You are blessed indeed and will be honored in this land forever."

And so for a time, Brendan and his companions remained in the Land of Promise and learned much wisdom thereby. At the end of that period they took leave of the bird, who chose to remain behind. Then they set sail for home, trusting to the rhythms of the sea to carry them where they needed to go.

The Death of Brendan

Thus they came home, without further adventure, and were welcomed by all. As they spoke of their voyage and word of it soon spread, Brendan and his companions became famous throughout Ireland and Britain, and Brendan himself traveled about, performing many miracles in the name of God.

And so the years passed until Brendan was ninety years old. One day when he was at a place named Enach Duin, there came to him a youth who was a bard and asked if he might play for the great man. At first Brendan would not let him, for he said that no music could be as fine as that which he had heard in the Land of Promise, which he continued to hear every day in his inner thoughts. But at last he relented and the youth played some strains of music. As he listened, tears gathered in Brendan's eyes and rolled down his aged cheeks.

When the youth had finished, Brendan thanked him. "Now I know that my death is near," he said. "For this is the music I have longed to hear." And when he looked again, the youth was nowhere to be seen.

Then Brendan called to the brethren who cared for him and told them that he would die in a few days. And so it was. Everything was done as Brendan had wished, and his remains were laid to rest in the shadow of a tree at Clonfert. Thereafter, many miracles were performed in his name, and all called him by the name of Saint Brendan. But of all the stories that are told of his deeds, none are better known, and rightly so, than that concerning his voyage in search of the Land of Promise.

These remarkable men who set forth, blindly and with little idea of where they were really going, are not hard to identify with. All they know is that their leader had been "called" by God's angel to find a "secret country" that holds the prospect of wonder and blessing. But the journey is not that simple. On the way they will visit a number of islands—places that represent some of the stages on the soul's journey—and on each one they will encounter something extraordinary, something that will change them forever. At the end of the voyage, when they return home, they are not the same people who left the shores of their own land in search of another.

Brendan himself is, from the start, gifted with inner certainty, a vision that not only makes him the natural leader of the company but gives him insight into all that takes place. In this he is like that part of us all that is heard when we are in need of advice—the "still, small voice" that tells us what we must do. Of course, we do not always listen, but to ignore the inner prompting is to court missed opportunity. Thus the story speaks to us of trust—for Brendan must trust his inner voice, just as his companions must trust his leadership.

From the start the voyagers are guided by otherworldly agents: the unseen people who care for them on the Island of Hospitality, the wonderful bird who speaks to them on three separate occasions, offering help and guidance when they need it most—even the mighty beast Jasconius, on whose back they almost celebrate Easter and who later on guides them toward the end of their voyage. Nor should we forget the magical otter who feeds the hermit Paul with a fish every day of his thirty-year sojourn on a tiny islet.

There are human helpers too: the Ageless Elders and the mysterious angelic beings who appear at odd moments along the way to guide and advise the voyagers—just as, in our own lives, friends or helpers appear at opportune times to offer us the gifts of friendship and timely advice. Indeed we are more gifted than we realize with moments we may call synchronous; events that, often only retrospectively, we perceive as guiding our own voyage through life.

Again and again, Brendan and his companions must give themselves up to the will of the waves, the rhythms of the ocean on whose back they sail, the guidance of the angel who, as Brendan says, is their navigator. It is these subtle rhythms, present also in the episode of the fish that seem to dance to a rhythm all their own, that offer us a pattern we can follow and learn from. We are like dancers ourselves, learning the steps and trying to follow the rhythm.

If one of the purposes of life is to find our appropriate course, then to be out of step with the universe is often a reason for our own failure to do so. Brendan and his companions constantly learn to accept the pattern that they are meant to follow—not slavishly and without freedom of choice, but simply by listening to and following the advice of those who have already been where they are headed and have experienced the difficulties of the voyage for themselves.

Often they are tested, just as we are, by the rigors of the journey. They, and we, must learn when to take what is offered and when to await permission: when to take only enough "food and water of the spirit," and when to be sensitive to the rhythms of the world in which we find ourselves, which has its own laws. We hear of the companions who drink too much of the water of the island and are lost in sleep as a result, or the man who steals the silver bridle and must pay the ultimate price for his action. Even here the meaning is metaphorical as well as literal: to steal from life itself—for instance, by deliberately warping a truth we recognize—is just as much of a crime as actual theft from others in the outer world.

There are mysteries as well, for the world is full of wonders and not everything is meant to be understood—the island of the crystal pillar, draped in the net through which it is hard to find a way, or the strange island of Smiths, where the fierce occupants are threatening to the voyagers. These are left unexplained but echo the mysterious adventures of the older voyagers, so that we know that they sail close to the borders of the Otherworld and are even able to look within for a moment. Such glimpses are as magical in our own lives as in the story—they are like the chinks of glorious light that sometimes pierce the soul's darker moments. They remind us also, just as the mariner Barinthus was told, that the Land of Promise represents a state that we have experienced before and that can be experienced again, if we so desire.

Throughout the story we are constantly told that the voyagers give themselves up to the rhythms of the natural world, for they are sailing the event horizon of creation, where anything may happen and frequently does. The soul's journey is just as magical—just as fraught with adventure and mystery—as Brendan's voyage. From it we learn to see the inner light that illumines everything, that makes us part of the continuing unfoldment of creation.

And if we listen carefully enough, we may hear things within this story that speaks to us at a deep level. Our own voyage may be only just beginning, or we may be nearing the harbor of the Land of Promise, but if we can learn to take soundings, to look about us with open eyes (how often do we think we see the truth only to find *later on that we were wrong?) and to watch the water of the ocean on which we are sailing, we are far more likely to find clues to understanding the direction in which we are moving.*

MEDITATION POINTS

- Consider you own life as a voyage. Where are you at present—at the beginning, nearing the end, or somewhere in between?

- What patterns are there that you are aware of that have shaped your life?

- If you had to describe your own journey in terms of the voyage, what island points have you passed through to reach your current place?

- Draw a map charting the islands on your own immram. Give them names and a brief description of what took place there—for example: "The Island of Earthly Delights." Here I met my future life partner and we fell in love.

- Ask yourself: What, in my life, is the light that never fails? Do I listen to my own inner voice or ignore it?

Columba's Song of the Ocean

Delightful would it be
To stand on a pinnacle of a rock—
That I might frequently see
The face of the ocean;
That I might hear the heaving waves
Chant their music to the Father;
That I might see the sparkling strand,
And hear the roar of the sea
By the Churchyard wall;
That I might see flocks of birds
Over the tumultuous ocean;
That I might see monsters
The greatest of its wonders;
That I might see its ebb and flow
In their going and coming;
That I might bless the King
Who created all: land, strand, and flood;
That I might search my books
For the good of my soul;
At times on my knees
To the King of Heaven;
At times fishing,
At times in my solitary cell.

(J.M., attributed to Columba)

...

TWO

THE BLACKBIRD'S CRY

KEVIN OF GLENDALOUGH
(June 3)

Where Kevin was the eagles came
Down from the highest mountains, tame,
And sat among the lesser birds
To hear the wisdom of his words,
The speckled trout would swiftly glide
To the reedy water's side . . .
Saint Kevin & the Wild Beasts: John Irvine

...

The companionship of beast and bird, insect and fish, lies at the heart of all Celtic spirituality, both pagan and Christian. Druids and saints alike knew that one could learn from those that flew or crawled, that walked on four feet, or that swam in water. Creaturely trust and fellowship all were important aspects of the life and beliefs of these early teachers, who regarded all living things as brothers and sisters, all a part of one creation under heaven, and their simple beauty as a reflection of the beauty of the otherworld.

As if in response to this, the creatures themselves became guides and helpers, just as they had been in the older, shamanic tradition, where any creature, be it eagle or mouse, could be a great spiritual teacher who had chosen this form for the sake of comfort and familiarity to those they helped. Again and again in the poetry of the times, this is emphasized, as in this poem where a monk is inspired by the "learned music" of the lark.

Learned in music sings the lark,

I leave my cell to listen:

His open beak spills music, hark!

Where heaven's bright cloudlets glisten.

Living a solitary existence, the Céli Dé had time to listen and were close enough to nature to appreciate both its terrors and its wonders. St. Kentigern followed a hound and a robin to the place where he was to found his monastery (see chapter 14); Piran of Cornwall founded a monastery in which the first monks were a fox, a badger, a wolf, and a doe, while Colman of Lindisfarne found support for his austere way of life from a cock, a mouse, and a fly. The cock and the mouse wakened him at prayer times, while the fly kept his place on the page he was reading whenever he was called away.

These are a remarkable enough testimony to the intimate relationship of human and creature, but in stories of Kevin of Glendalough, who was born in Leinster around the middle of the sixth century, we find this magnified to a degree seldom equaled anywhere else. The site of the monastery may still be seen, in the shadow of the Wicklow Mountains, a few miles south of Dublin.

A Beautiful Shining Birth

Kevin was born of royal blood in the Fort of the White Fountain. His parents, Caemlug and Caemell, knew of a prophecy that spoke of the coming of one especially blessed, who would bring great goodness and well-being to the province of Leinster. But Caemell had no suspicion that it was to be her fourth son who would fulfill this promise, until, as she lay in childbed, she received a visitation from one of the Shining Ones who are called angels, who told her that she should give the name Coemgen, "beautiful, shining birth," to the son she would shortly bear, but that afterward he would have another name.

And so the child was born, an easy birth without pain, and when the day came for him to be baptized it was said that no fewer than twelve Shining Ones attended upon him, singing praises around him and prophesying his greatness, but his mother said afterward that she heard only the cry of a blackbird that flew into the church and sat in the rafters, singing its own glorious song. Cronan, one of the holiest men in Leinster, performed the baptismal ceremony and named the child Kevin, for that was the name of which prophesy had spoken. And when the child's parents questioned him, Cronan closed his eyes and answered with this inspired verse:

This name, fashioned in heaven,
Shall cling to the child:
Believe, O woman of fair attendance,
that this shall be his given name.

...

Kevin's family took the baby home to the Fort of the White Fountain. Next day, as his mother sat with him at her breast, a white cow appeared, of great beauty, which had never been seen before. When she saw it, Caemell knew that it had been sent by the Lady Bridget herself to feed her child. Every day thereafter for the next year it came, and Kevin drank of its milk until he was weaned, after which the cow vanished without a trace and was never seen again.

Thus Kevin grew until he was seven years old, at which time he saw a shining figure that spoke to him and told him to enter a monastery, where he might learn all that was required to become a wise and honorable teacher. Despite his youth, Kevin convinced his parents that the message of the Shining One should be obeyed, and the serious child grew to be a serious youth among the monks, who grew to love him for his gentleness and kindness to all living things. It was at this time that he made many friends among the wild animals and birds that lived around about the monastery. And often a solitary blackbird came and perched outside the window of his cell and sang to him.

One day the novice master ordered Kevin to bring fire with which to light the candles in the church, and Kevin asked if he could have a vessel in which to carry the hot coals. For some reason the novice master became angry at this and ordered Kevin to carry them in the corner of his cloak. Without hesitating, Kevin went away and returned shortly after with several red-hot coals gathered into his mantle, and not even a scorch mark was there to see when he laid them by the alter. When he saw this, the novice master said, "Indeed you are a child of wonder. I truly believe that all the prophecies that were made of you will be fulfilled."

Life in the Wild World

Soon after this, Kevin had a vision. A Shining One came to him and told him to go into a lonely place named Glendaloch. Kevin did as his vision bade him, and found a cave in which to live. And in time to come, this place was known as "Kevin's Bed" because he had slept there.

This was a hard time for him, for he forsook the companionship of his fellow men utterly and lived in the wild, dressing in animal skins and sleeping on a stone bed. For food he ate nuts and herbs and other wild plants that nourished him. He had no fire to warm him and often went to the lonely loch at the head of the valley and stood waist deep in the icy water for hours until he entered a state in which he saw the realm of the spirits clearly and spoke with the Shining Ones and other beings, who were as real to him as any man or woman.

One day he sat by the edge of the loch reading from a most precious book of holy words, which was his only possession. The cold numbed his hands and he let slip the book, which fell into the lake. For a while, Kevin sat numbed with sorrow, then a sleek head broke the surface of the water. It was an otter, and in its mouth was his book. Kevin took it and opened it and saw that not a single word was blotted. He thanked the otter and thereafter always shared some of his food with it. Sometimes the otter brought him fish, and they would share this as friends will.

Always Kevin sought to live alone, as far away from people as he could. But he knew in his heart that one day he must return to the world of men and begin to teach the wisdom he had learned through living in the wild world.

One day he went to a part of the valley where there was a deep woods, and there he lived for a time, listening to the slow, ancient voices of the trees and the songs of the birds that nested there. Here he heard the voice of the blackbird every day and grew to know every note of its song. Then there came a day when he was lying down in a hollow scraped in the bare earth, when a cow appeared suddenly at his side and began to lick his feet. Kevin laid his hands upon the gentle beast and drew close to share in her warmth.

Unbeknown to Kevin, the cow belonged to a farmer named Dimma, who pastured his animals in the forest and the surrounding land. At the end of the day the beast rejoined the rest of the herd and went home to Dimma's farm. There, to everyone's puzzlement, she gave as much milk as the rest of the herd put together. After this, every time the herd went to the forest, the same cow would seek out the place here Kevin lay and remain with him throughout the day. And every time it was the same: the cow returned home and gave such generous portions of milk that everyone was astonished.

Finally, Dimma ordered his herdsman to follow the cow and see where it went. The man obeyed and found Kevin, lying thin and wasted from his life in the wild, barely able to stand or speak. Kevin so longed to be apart from other men that he begged the herdsman not to reveal his secret, and at first the man gave his word. But when he returned to the farm, Dimma questioned him so closely that in the end he gave way and told his master everything he had seen.

At once the farmer knew that this must be the holy man who was rumored to live in lonely Glendalough, and he swore that he would bring Kevin back to his house. "For surely he will bring good fortune upon us all," said Dimma. "It is not right that so good a man should live alone and neglected when he is so close to human habitation."

So the farmer called his children to him, and they made a litter of tree branches and set off to the woods to find Kevin. When they did so, he was so weak that he could not stand, and so they lifted him into the litter, where he lay quietly and without complaint, having understood that the time was come for him to reenter the world.

On the way home the woods were so thick and impenetrable that they found it difficult to get through with the litter. But when he saw this, Kevin prayed to the Shining Ones and the trees drew apart on either side until they had passed, only then resuming their former stance.

The Blackbird

Thus Kevin returned home to Dimma's farm and was nursed back to health and strength. And in return for his blessing and the wisdom he shared with everyone, the farmer built him a tiny cell in the woods, where he could live as he wished, and where those who wished could seek him out. And indeed many came, as word of the holy man's wisdom spread throughout Leinster and beyond.

It was Kevin's habit to sit for long hours in his cell, with arms outstretched. And because the wattled hut was so very small, this meant that both his hands were extended outside the tiny windows, made to let in the sun and the winds. One day as he sat thus, rapt in contemplation of the divine world, a hen blackbird flew down and landed upon one of his hands as if it were the branch of a tree. All day the bird stayed, and Kevin remained unmoving.

Next day it was the same, and this time the bird began to bring tufts of hair and grass and sticks with which to make a nest. A smile lit Kevin's face like the sun, and he remained perfectly still as the bird prepared her nest. Soon there were eggs in the nest, and still Kevin kept still, sleeping on his feet and eating only when pilgrims came to visit him. These he bade keep silent and watch the bird, in whose daily actions were contained all the mystery and wonder of the world. Thus he kept alive, sustained more often by his love of the world alone, until the eggs hatched and the chicks left the nest.

On that day, one of the Shining Ones visited Kevin and told him that it was time for him to go out into the world and to build a foundation where others could come and learn. At first he resisted even this great demand, saying that he required longer to contemplate and learn the ways of all things. But the Shining One would brook no refusal, and so with reluctance Kevin came forth and began to seek those who would come together to form a community. Plenty there were who wished to share in his great wisdom and holiness, and soon there began to grow up in the lonely valley of Glendalough a monastery that would in time rival even Clonmacnoise. Indeed it was said that the four truly great places of pilgrimage in the whole of Ireland were the Cave of Patrick in Ulster, Croagh Patrick in Connacht, Inis na me-Beo (that is, the Land of the Living) in Munster, and Glendalough in Leinster.

So famous indeed did Kevin's foundation become that he was often hard pressed to feed those who came there. Even the herd of sheep with which he was gifted by farmers from Leinster and beyond was scarcely enough. Then the day came when Kevin was forced to turn away some beggars who had come in search of food. But even as they were preparing to depart, Kevin called them back. In the belief that a way would be found, he slaughtered the last few sheep in his flock and sent the beggars away happy. Next day the flock was renewed, exactly to the same number as before.

The Otter's Tale

Ever since the otter had brought back Kevin's book from the bottom of the lake, it had been wont to bring the gift of a fish. Every day it came to a certain point along the shore and left the fish for Kevin or one of his monks to find. Then one day it came no more, and Kevin went to the water's edge and called out to it to tell him why it had forgotten them. But the otter came not, and so Kevin went back to his church and prayed that he should be told what had happened to his faithful friend. Next day, Cellach, the son of the farmer Dimma who had long ago brought Kevin from the forest, came and confessed that he had tried to capture the otter, believing that its skin would bring profit to the monastery. At once, Kevin took the man back to the lakeside and made him promise, out loud, that he would never proffer harm to the otter or its kin, either then or at any time in the future. Next day the otter was back, and from then until the end of its days it continued to bring a fish for the monks.

The Doe and the Wolf

The king of Ui Faelain had an ongoing struggle with an evil witch. Every child born to him was stolen away or destroyed by her, and there was nothing he could do to prevent it. Then, when a new child, a son, was born to him, he hit upon the idea of sending him to be fostered by Kevin of Glendalough, believing that the power of the holy man would protect his offspring against any dark magic.

As soon as the child was old enough to be baptized, his father sent him to Kevin. And on the day of his baptism, the dark witch came with her followers, their ragged black clothes whipping in a wind that none other could feel. When he saw them coming, Kevin held up his hand against them, and they were at once turned to stone. To this day the stones may be seen clustered by the side of the lake.

So Kevin took in the infant son of the king, but at that time there were no cattle in the valley, and Kevin was concerned how he might obtain milk for the child. Then, just as had happened long ago when the white cow came to feed Kevin himself, so now came a white doe and her fawn. Every day the doe would come to a certain hollowed-out stone, and there she would drop her milk for her own offspring, and for the king's son also, who thrived upon it.

Then one day a wolf came hunting and caught and killed the fawn. Seeing this, Kevin bade the wolf offer no further threat to the doe, but to be quiet and lie down beside her as though it were her child. To the wonder of all, the wolf obeyed, and the doe continued to drop her milk at the hollowed-out stone until it was no longer needed. And in time the king's son grew up and became one of Kevin's most devoted followers.

The Hunted Boar

As time passed and the foundation of Glendalough grew in size and renown, Kevin sought often to return to his old hut in the wilds, often spending several weeks there before returning to the monastery. One day as he was sitting in the shade of the trees at the edge of the forest, meditating upon the wonders of the world, there came a great crashing and crying in the woods, and a wild boar burst out into the open and ran straight into Kevin's tiny cell. Almost at once a pack of savage hounds emerged from the trees in hot pursuit. When he saw them, Kevin called out to them to stop, and at once their feet became stuck to the ground.

A few moments later the huntsman himself, a fierce man named Brandub who was known as a killer of animals and men for sport, came into view. When he saw the dogs standing still around the hut where the boar still sheltered, he raised his whip. Then he caught sight of Kevin, sitting quietly beneath the trees with birds fluttering around him and sitting on his head and hands. When the hunters' eyes met those of the holy man, a change came over him, and he fell on his knees before Kevin and begged forgiveness for all he had done. Kevin forgave him, and the hounds were set free and went off with their master as gently as lambs. The boar remained in the woods and often visited with Kevin from that time on.

And so the days turned to years, and Kevin grew old. He lived long past the age reached by men at that time, and was loved and revered throughout the land of Ireland and beyond. The foundation at Glendalough became one of the most famous in all the Western world, and when Kevin died at last, many hundreds of pilgrims came to pay their respects. But as many as there were of humankind, so too were there animals and birds who came to bear witness to the understanding of the saint. And it is said that a single blackbird sat upon his grave for many days and visited it often thereafter.

The importance of animals in everyday Celtic culture was considerable, and there are a number of stories that show that Kevin's relationship with animals and birds was a not-uncommon tradition among older, pre-Christian figures. In some of the earliest Celtic traditions that have survived, we hear of tribal shamans who were either transformed into animals or possessed animal "helpers," otherworldly spirits who took the form of beasts, birds, or fish and were able to act as guides though both their own particular element. In each case the shaman sought to take on the natural abilities of the creature itself: the strength of the bear, the speed of the hare, the keen-sightedness of the eagle or the hawk. By adopting the shape and consciousness of the creaturely, the shaman projected himself outside the normal range of human awareness, into a world where everything was different: more balanced, less complicated, less bound by the laws and mores of his own world. From here he could view the world of mortals and perceive it more clearly, with the kind of insights not generally available to him.

An early story that could easily have been told of Kevin relates how a man called Marvan possessed a white boar that he declared to be "a herdsman, a physician . . . and a musician." When asked how this was possible, Marvan replied: "When I return from [herding] the swine at night, and the skin is torn off my feet by the briars of Glen-a-Scail, he comes to me and rubs his tongue over my foot, and he goes after the swine. . . . He is a musician to me, for when I am anxious to sleep I give him a stroke with my foot, and he lies on his back with his belly uppermost and sings me a humming tune, and his music is more grateful to me than that of a sweet-toned harp in the hands of an accomplished minstrel." The boar, like most of the creatures mentioned in Kevin's story, was sacred to the Celts.

Animals were frequently twinned with human births, so that the resulting offspring became closely allied in later life. The Welsh hero Pwyll is stolen from his mother's side by a monster and left in a stable with a newborn colt that afterward plays a significant part in his life. The fate of the Irish warrior Cuchulainn was linked with dogs (his name means "Hound of Culainn"), and it was only after he had been tricked into eating dogmeat that he was finally killed. It was also said of Cuchulainn that a mare dropped twin foals on the night of his birth, and that these became famous as the Black Saighlenn and Macha's Grey, with whom Cuchulainn had an almost symbiotic connection and which arose from the depths of a lake at his call.

Another important role attributed to animals was their ability to provide inspiration, or to possess a knowledge of the past that far outstripped that of a human. Some creatures were believed to live to very great ages or were anyway of otherworldly provenance and thus possessed of wisdom deeper than that of mortals. In the story of "The Hawk of Achill," we see this as part of a theme known as "The Oldest Animals," where a number of creatures are consulted about various things and refer the questioner to successively more-ancient beings.

In the story there is a wonderful dialogue between the wise Druid Fintan and the hawk of the title, part of which reads as follows:

Fintan

Relate now, O bird of Achill,
The substance of your adventures;
For I am able finally
To converse in your tongue.

The Bird
Though you seem still young,
It is long since you became shrunken,
In Dun Tulera washed by the sea,
O Fintan, O wise man.

Fintan
O bird of Achill of the Fian,
Whom I have long desired to see,
Now that you are here indeed, tell me
Why you cleave to Achill?

The Bird
O Fintan, never was there
A single night in Achill,
When I failed to obtain by my strength
Fish, game and venison.
O son of Bochra, speak fair,
And, since we are able to converse

Tell me of your life. . .

•••

A similar poem, found in a medieval Irish manuscript, tells the story of the White Blackbird. Enaccan, an old bard, asks a blackbird what has whitened its wing down one side, and the bird replies that it was Christ, who had kept it alive for longer than its normally allotted span (we are not told why this should have happened). The bird then proceeds to relate various events it had witnessed in its long life.

He speaks of King Conchobar and the great gatherings of the Ultonians in ancient days; of Queen Maeve and her expedition on the Tain bo Cualnge. Far from him now was the vigour of these gatherings, for he is older than Ross son of Ruadh [tutor to Cuchulainn]. He has met with Oisin, son of Fionn, a man of wisdom. . . . He had witnessed the birth of Christ in the flesh. Sweet was his song from the Wood of Cuan when the host was destroying Troy. Many had been his adventures since Bran went away on his ship . . . (The Book of Fermoy)

The most important single factor in these stories is that all the protagonists are carriers of tradition. They all remember a past so old that no human mind can encompass it. Nor is it just the facts of history they relate, but the mysterious, inner tradition of the land. In this way the past is kept alive, and its representatives become living containers for an accumulation of knowledge. Much of the wisdom stored up in the lives of the Celtic saints is of this kind, and like the older poetic and mythical stories to which they are akin, they form an index to the traditions, rites, and beliefs of the Celtic peoples.

There is much that we, too, can learn from the creatures we encounter in our daily lives. Whether it is a beloved pet, a chance encounter with a creature in the wild, or coming face to face with another species in a zoo, we may be struck not only by the otherness of the being we face, but also of the links, at a soul level, that connect us. From the very beginning of recorded history, an almost symbiotic relationship has existed between humankind and the animal kingdom. The earliest representations of animals in the cave art left behind by the Neanderthal people show that even in the pursuit of the creatures for food, the hunter took upon him something of the nature of the creature itself. In shamanic tradition all over the world, the same intimate spiritual connection still holds true, and to a lesser degree the same holds good for our own relationship with our pets. Anyone who has looked into the eyes of dog or cat sees a mystery reflected back at them—something that extends beyond words, beyond even feelings, into the regions of the soul where all things share a common creaturehood. Even if we have never had a pet in our lives, we may well find that a casual meeting with a bird or beast while out walking can have a deep and lasting effect upon us. The mind remembers a fleeting glimpse of a deer or stag, caught for a moment in the headlight of a car before leaping away. The heart understands birdsong better than the head and responds with feelings of joy or sadness according to circumstance and song.

The kind of relationship described in the story of Kevin may be rare, but it is by no means impossible in our own time. The beasts who attended upon the saint felt the innate goodness of his soul; we do not need to aspire to holiness to extend the friendship of the soul to all creatures, and when we do so, the rewards are great. For a brief time we can see with the eyes of the hawk, swim with the motion of the fish, hear the blood pounding in the heart of the stag. Again and again, Kevin reaches out to a creature of fur, fin, or feather and is rewarded with a depth of response that is not hard to imagine. The strength, tenacity, grace, and beauty of all creatures is ours to access if we meet them on equal terms. This is the true meaning of the idea that mankind was given "dominion" over the animal world, not that we should dominate, command, or enslave as we have so often done in the past and continue, distressingly, to do today. Rather, the intent was that we should learn to live at one with our environment, of which the creatures are a hugely important part. When we are able to see this clearly, and to give up experimenting on living creatures or enslaving them for food and well-being, we shall once again begin to experience the relationship that was once as natural as the sunrise to us all. At a personal level we can do this already, by simply tuning in to the creatures who share our planet, and coming to terms with the fact that they are just as important as us.

MEDITATION POINTS

- Consider any animal, bird, fish, or insect with which you have had a direct encounter: How did this feel? Were you afraid, angry, loving, awed?

- If you have pets and do not already do so, spend some time interacting with them every day at a specific time.

- Consider what it might feel like to be an animal living in the wild.

- Now consider what it feels like to be a domesticated animal, whether in the home or on the farm.

- Ask yourself what you can do to change the lot of any creature that is suffering from the actions of our own species.

Pangur Ban

I and Pangur Ban my cat,
'Tis a like task we are at:
Hunting mice is his delight
Hunting words I sit all night.

Better far than praise of men
'Tis to sit with book and pen;
Pangur bears me no ill will,
He too plies his simple skill.

'Tis a merry thing to see
At our tasks how glad are we,
When at home we sit and find
Entertainment to our mind.

Oftentimes a mouse will stray
In our hero Pangur's way;
Oftentimes my keen thought set
Takes a meaning in its net.
'Gainst the wall he set his eye
Full and fierce and sharp and sly;
Gainst the wall of knowledge I
All my little wisdom try.

When a mouse darts from its den
O how glad is Pangur then!
O what gladness do I prove
When I solve the doubts I love!

So in peace our tasks we ply,
Pangur Ban, my cat, and I;
In our arts we find our bliss,
I have mine and he has his.

Practice every day has made
Pangur perfect in his trade;
I get wisdom day and night
Turning darkness into light.

(Verses written on the border of a manuscript;
translated by Robin Flower)

...

THREE

ALL THE BRIGHT BLESSINGS

BRIGHID OF KILDARE
(February 2)

The genealogy of the holy maiden Bride,
Radiant flame of gold, noble foster mother of Christ.
Bride the daughter of Dougal the Brown,
Son of Aodh, son of Art, son of Conn,
Son of Criara, son of Cairpre, son of Cas,
Son of Cormac, son of Cartach, son of Conn.

—Genealogy of Bride from *The Carmina Gadelica*

•••

Brighid's life is marked out by divine fire. Again and again, we hear of a burning light that surrounded her or gathered above her head. Even her name has been interpreted as deriving from brea-aigit, "fiery arrow." She is arguably one of the greatest spiritual figures of early Ireland, and the facts about her life can be briefly summarized, but her influence is far more wide reaching. As a woman in a world dominated by men—as much in spiritual circles as secular—she was a powerful influence on both men and women. Indeed, it has been often noted that one of the truly original aspects of Celtic Christianity was its openness to the feminine. A ninth-century text, the "Catalogue of the Saints in Ireland," makes this clear when it says that the founders of the Celtic church "did not reject the service and society of women." Brighid herself founded one of the first "double" monasteries at Kildare, where both men and women lived in separate, adjacent quarters and came together in a single church to worship. There were a number of such foundations in Britain and Ireland at this time, and more than two hundred women saints are listed in the life of Gorman, the oldest female saint of whom we have any knowledge.

Brighid herself was born in the province of Leinster and lived from around 452 to 524. Called "the Mary of the Gael" in token of her importance, she inherited many of the aspects of one of the great goddess figures of the Celts, Brighid, who was the deity of poetry, smithcraft, and the hearth. It may have been this that promoted the numerous references to fire in her story, and she shared her feast day, February 1, with the earlier figure. Her followers kept an eternal flame burning in the monastery she founded at Kildare, a custom properly inherited from an older college of Druids who occupied the same before her. In our own time, these fires, which were finally extinguished only during the sixteenth-century Reformation, have been relit by women of many different cultures and beliefs, so that even now the eternal flame of Brighid's heart is burning to fuel our own voyages in search of inner light.

Brighid is a supreme example of the kind of crossover between traditions that occurred during this time, a linking of the old and new beliefs, which frequently existed side by side and in harmony. The earliest version of Brighid's life, on which the following story is based, makes it clear that Druids and Christians had far more in common than is generally understood, and that there were evident parallels in their approach to spirituality.

Brighid's compassionate nature, her openness to other kinds of belief, and, above all, the burning passion of her spirituality make her one of the most important characters of the Celtic world. Known in Scotland as Bride, in Ireland as Brighid, in Wales as San Ffraid, and in Britain as Brigantia, she is the major exemplar of the marriage of the old and the new, the pagan and the Christian. Her story is about offering the entire harvest of a life lived to the full, of a love expressed for every part of creation.

There was a nobleman in Leinster called Dubhthach, who acquired a bondwoman named Broetsech. She was gentle and pretty, so that Dubhthach evinced a liking for her and took her to his bed. Soon after, it became evident that she was with child, and when Dubhthach's wife learned that he was the father of the child, she was not best pleased.

"Get rid of her," she said, "for I fear that one day her seed shall rule mine."

Dubhthach was unwilling to do this, for he had come to love Broetsech, but his wife made it clear that she would not let the matter rest. Then, while he struggled with the decision that must be made, an event took place that changed everything.

One day Dubhthach rode out in his chariot with Broetsech at his side. As they went, they happened to pass the house of a certain Druid who, when he heard the chariot coming, asked his servant to go out and discover who it was that was coming. "For I believe it is a king who comes."

When the servant returned and told him it was only Dubhthach, the Druid came out to look for himself. When he saw the bondwoman standing beside Dubhthach, he looked at her with the eye of vision and asked, "Are you with child?" When Broetsech admitted that she was, the Druid asked, "And who is the father?"

"It is I who am the father," answered Dubhthach.

"Then take great care of this woman, for she has conceived a wondrous child."

"My wife wants me to sell her," said Dubhthach, "fearing that her seed shall be greater than her own."

"That is true," said the Druid. "Her children shall serve the children of this woman in generations to come. But do not fear," he went on, speaking to Broetsech. "Soon you shall give birth to a daughter whose radiance shall outshine the sun. No one shall harm you or your child, for there is a strong protection about you that none may overcome."

Now Dubhthach was even more determined not to sell his bondwoman, despite the pressure that both his wife and her brothers brought upon him. And so matters continued until one day it happened that a poet of the O'Neills happened to be staying in Dubhthach's house, and when he learned something of the anger that was between Dubhthach and his wife, he offered to buy Broetsech and to care for her.

"Very well," said Dubhthach with a sigh, "But understand this: the child in her womb is mine and belongs to me."

So Broetsech went home with the poet, who treated her well enough. Then one day soon after, a Druid came to stay in the poet's house, and he awoke in the middle of the night and saw that over the bondwoman stood a pillar of flame that lit up the night until it was as bright as day. No one else saw this, but next morning the Druid came to the poet and asked if he might buy the bondwoman from him. The poet agreed but said, "The child she will bear belongs to Dubhthach of Leinster. See that no harm comes to it."

"Of that you may be certain," said the Druid.

Broetsech went with him that same day, for it was evident that she must soon bring forth her child, but at this time she was still able to travel.

Now it happened that soon after this, the Druid made a great feast and invited the king of Connaught and his queen, who herself went heavy with child. And that night at the feast, the king asked when an auspicious time for his queen might be to bear their son. The Druid looked into the place within and said, "If she gives birth before sunrise, neither within or without this house, the child she bears will grow to be among the greatest in all of Ireland."

But as it happened, the queen came to her term that very night, and the child she bore was stillborn. But in the morning, when Broetsech was returning from the milking parlor with a pail of fresh milk, she had put only one foot across the threshold when she fell down and, there and then, gave birth to her child. The

Druid's servants came to help her, and they bathed the child in the milk that her mother had but lately drawn. And some say that the baby was taken and laid next to the queen's dead son, and that he began to breath at that moment, but whether this is true or not I cannot say, only that Broetsech's child was passing fair to look upon, and that from the moment of her birth she seemed to shine with a light that was not of mortal origin.

First Miracles

So for a time, Broetsech and her child continued to live under the Druid's roof. Once the bondwoman had recovered from her lying-in, she returned to her duties. So it was that one day she went out to the milking and left her daughter sleeping in the house. Passing neighbors saw the house in flames from ground to roof and ran for help. Yet, when they returned with water there was no sign of any fire, and the child slept peacefully in her cradle. The Druid, when he heard of this, said that it showed how the child burned with an inner fire that would one day be seen throughout Ireland. Soon after that, he dreamed a dream in which three shining figures came and baptized the child in the name of Brighid, which means "fiery arrow." When he told her mother this, the bondwoman declared that thus would she name her child, and the Druid said that since the Shining Ones themselves desired it, so it should be, and that her name was a foretelling of her life.

Thereafter the Druid took an special interest in the child and watched her often. He noticed, as did all, that as she grew so she ate less. Whatever was put before her from the Druid's table she could not stomach but vomited it up. When he saw this, the Druid looked into the Place Within and declared that the child should take milk from a certain red-eared cow in his herd and bade a woman named Christina to milk it daily and to be Brighid's nurse thereafter. This milk Brighid was able to take, and afterward she grew daily more hale and strong.

As time passed, Brighid began to ask about her father, and learning that he was the noble Dubhthach, she wished to go and see him. The Druid sent word, and, filled with pride when he heard of the extraordinary nature of his daughter, Dubhthach came to bring her home to Leinster. On the journey, Brighid's nurse, who had come with her, fell ill. Hearing of a certain lord who was holding a great feast nearby, Brighid and another girl in the party went to beg some ale for the sick woman. The lord refused them. Brighid therefore went to a nearby well and, having drawn water, said a blessing over it, at which it took on both the appearance and taste of ale. She took this back to the sick woman, who began to recover as soon as she drank. But as to the lord's feast, when they opened the barrels of ale that had been set aside for it, they were found to be dry.

Amazed and somewhat bemused by this evidence of his daughter's wondrous gifts, Dubhthach gave her the task of looking after the swine. One time when he was away, robbers came and stole two of the pigs. By chance, Dubhthach encountered them upon the road and was able to take back what they had stolen. When he returned, he put the pigs into a pen on their own, then he went to Brighid and said, "Are all the swine safe?" Brighid looked at him solemnly and said, "Do you go and count them, father." And when Dubhthach did so, there was exactly the right number.

Whatever Brighid did seemed to turn to increase. One time when Dubhthach had a noble guest, he gave to his daughter the task of preparing a meal. She was given five strips of bacon to cook and set about it while the guest nodded before the fire. She had scarcely begun when a poor hungry hound entered the house and begged for food. Brighid at once gave it one of the strips of bacon, and when that was not enough, a second strip. Soon Dubhthach came and asked her if the supper was ready. Brighid laid out five strips of bacon for the guest, who looked with wonder upon the feast. Then he told Dubhthach how he had seen the girl feed the hungry dog. After that, neither felt like eating the food but instead gave it to be shared among the poor.

Soon after this, Bridgid returned to the Druid's house to see her mother and found Broetsech ill with a fever. The bondwoman's task at that time consisted of looking after the dairy and making butter for the household. Brighid took over this task with a will and performed her duties so well that the amount of butter produced by the dairy more than doubled. The Druid decided to discover if this was another of the girl's miraculous works, so he took a huge basket to the dairy and asked Brighid if she could fill it. Now at that moment, she had only enough to fill a quarter of the basket, but she went into the kitchen and uttered a charm over the butter.

O great prince,
Who can do everything,
Bless, O God,
My kitchen with your right hand.

My kitchen,
A kitchen of the White God
A kitchen my King has blessed—
A kitchen filled with butter!

...

The Druid heard this and wondered. When the girl came out to him, she had enough butter to fill another third of the basket, but somehow, when she placed it inside, it grew to fill the whole. When he saw this, the Druid said, "Truly you are most wondrous." Then he offered to give her cattle for her own. But Brighid shook her head. "I have no need of cattle, but if you wish to reward me, then give my mother her freedom."

The Druid answered, "It shall be as you wish. But you shall have the cattle also, and anything else that I can spare."

Thus Brighid and her mother returned home to Leinster and to her father's house. And at first, all was well with them. But then there came a suitor who desired to marry Dubhthach's daughter, and he was more than willing. But Brighid said that she would never marry, since she had other work to do. Dubhthach was angry at that and threatened to sell her, since by law she was still his property. But Brighid looked at him and said, "If you force this upon me, I shall pluck out my eyes, for I will never be wife to any man!" Such was the fire in her then, that Dubhthach could not gainsay her, and soon after he gave her her freedom.

Brighid the Abbess

For a time, Brighid and her mother lived together, eking out their livelihood from the cattle the Druid had given them. Then one day Brighid announced that she intended to join a community of holy women in Telch Mide. "For I have seen that I have work to do in this world, and thus will it begin."

So Brighid went to Bishop Mél, who, having heard something of her remarkable abilities, was glad to welcome her. It is said that on the night before she arrived, the bishop dreamed a dream of the Mother of God, and that when he saw Brighid face to face, she bore the same appearance as the woman in his dream. For which reason, it is told that Brighid in after years was known as "the Mary of the Gaelic People."

When the day appointed for her to take the veil arrived, Bridgid waited with several other women who all were to dedicate themselves to the service of God. When Brighid's turn came, it happened that the prelate read out the wrong form of words over her; namely, that for an abbess. When it was realized what he had done, there was an instant outcry, for many present believed that a woman could not hold so high an office. But at that moment they all saw a column of flame enfold Brighid, and in awe Bishop Mél declared that a higher authority than his had chosen Brighid for this role.

Thus it came about that Brighid became an abbess, though she was scarcely twenty-two and had as yet no foundation or following. Yet, word of the wonders that followed her quickly spread. It was told how she cured lepers and the blind, and how a young boy who had been dumb from birth spoke when she asked him a question. Even her shadow was said to heal others, and water or milk blessed by her wrought miracles. Above all, it was the increase of all things that people spoke of. Whether sheep or cattle or pigs, food or ale or wheat, whenever there was an insufficiency of these things among any community in need, if Brighid came there it was sure to be sufficient and more.

And so it came to be that a large number of men and women came seeking her, wishing both to be in her presence and to hear her teachings. When she saw this, Brighid sent word to Bishop Mél, asking him to come with her in search of a site on which she could build her own foundation. For a time, they traveled together and found nowhere suitable. Then, on a certain day as they were on the road, they met a cavalcade of carts loaded with wood that were destined for Ailill, son of Dunlang. Now when Brighid saw this, she looked within and listened to the voice of an unseen companion. When she had heard all there was to hear, she went to Ailill and asked if she might have some of the wood with which to build at a spot near there.

"Not so much as a stick will I give to you," Ailill declared. As he spoke, all the carts came to a halt in the road, and the horses could not take another step nor be moved by any means. When he saw this, Ailill bowed to Brighid and begged her to take all the wood she wished.

Thus the building began at a place nearby, which was known as Kildare and had previously housed a community of Druids. Brighid was especially glad to be here, feeling the commonality of all beliefs, and here she founded her first community, which was to become one of the foremost in all of Ireland. And the first thing that Brighid caused to be done when the building was complete was the lighting of a fire on the chief hearthstone of the foundation, and when it was alight, she said, "May this light burn forever in the world and may it never be allowed to go out." And both while she was alive and for many years after her death, the fire was tended in such a way that it was never extinguished.

The Wounded Healer

Not long after this, Brighid fell ill, being affected by a disease of the eyes and headaches that made her unable to stand. Bishop Mél came to her and would have taken her to a famous healer who lived some way away. They set forth, Brighid riding with difficulty. Along the way, Brighid became dizzy and fell from the horse's back and onto the road. Her head struck a stone, and the wound bled profusely. She was helped to mount again, and they continued on until they reached the place where the healer lived. When he saw the abbess, he said that there was no greater source of healing than herself, and that he could do nothing for her. When he spoke these words, the sickness left Brighid and she was as hale as ever—though afterward it was said that she saw things in the inner worlds more clearly than before and was herself an even more powerful healer.

On the way back to Kildare, Brighid and the bishop stayed for a night in the house of the king of Teffia. It happened that a servant broke a most precious cup that belonged to the king, for which he was thrown into prison. When Brighid heard of this, she asked that he be set free, but the king refused her. "Then give me the shards of the cup," requested Brighid. "Those you may have," said the king. When Brighid took them in her hands and breathed upon them, they were restored as if they had never been broken. "Thus is the life of the soul," Brighid said. "Though it may be easily broken, yet it may be restored." At this the king sent word to release his servant, and he became a devoted follower of Brighid thereafter.

This was not the only time that Brighid saved a condemned man. Once when she was in the district of Fir Rois, she heard of a man who had been imprisoned for no good reason. She begged the local king for his release. "Not though you offered me the sun and the moon," said he. "But so that you shall not go from here with a refusal, I give you the care of his soul for one night."

At that, Brighid smiled and went to the man in prison. There she taught him some words of blessing and said to him, "When you say these, your chains shall fall from you." Wondering, the man did as he was bid and the chains fell from him. "Now," said Brighid, "repeat the words once more, and when you do so the locks that hold you shall open." Again the man did as Brighid said, and the locks of his cell opened at once. "Now go home," said Brighid, and the man departed and was seen no more in that part of the country.

The Midwife of God

Brighid's fame continued to spread, and many more tales are told of her wondrous works. On one occasion it is said that when seven holy men came to visit her, there was insufficient milk to feed them all, for the cows had already been milked that day. But one of the Shining Ones that are called angels came to Brighid and told her to milk the cows again. When she did so, they gave enough milk for her guests, and moreover the milk continued to flow from the pails in which it was put, so that a river of milk spread out and formed a lake. This may still be seen today and is known still as the Lake of Milk.

Another time, a foolish churl in the service of the king of Leinster killed a tame fox that was much beloved of his lord and had been taught various tricks. When the king heard what had happened, he commanded that the man be thrown into prison. "Unless a fox as wise and skillful as mine comes to the court in the next few days," the king declared, "both this man and all his family shall be sold into slavery."

When word of this came to Brighid, she at once called for her chariot to be brought and set out for the king's court. As she went, she called aloud to all the creatures of the world to send her help. Soon there came a wild fox that ran beside her and finally jumped up and hid beneath her cloak. Thus Brighid came before the king and asked for the man to be set free. The king repeated his oath, and at that, Brighid opened her cloak and the fox jumped out and began to dance and pay tricks just as the old one had done. When he saw that, the king was well pleased and set free the man and his family, who went home with Brighid. Afterward, when they were safely away, the fox ran off and returned to the wild.

But one story is told that is a greater mystery than all the rest. For it is said that by some miraculous shifting of the shape of time, Brighid was permitted to pass for a time into the age when the Lord of the Elements was born. And it is told that she was at the lying-in of Mary and acted as midwife to the Child of Wonder. Whether this be a true tale or not, I cannot say, but it is told still in Ireland, and many there believe it to be so.

At length, the ending of her days came upon Brighid. Her last act was to ask again that the fires that burned on the hearthstones of Kildare be kept burning perpetually in token of the fires she had lit in the hearts of so many. And thus it was done, and thus it continues to be done even to this very time.

Many came to look upon her body and to honor her. And no lesser person than Colmcille himself made a song over her, which is still said to this day. And it is further said that when years after he was in danger upon the sea and spoke the words of his hymn aloud, the waters were calmed. This is the song that he made:

> *Brighid, excellent woman, flame of the sun,*
> *golden, delightful, radiant as the stars—*
> *may her dazzling light guide us to the long home,*
> *may she save us from all harm,*
> *may she fight our battles against disease,*
> *may the gentle rain of her spirit fall upon us!*

Brighid's story is about compassion and continuity—the compassion for all things that she constantly exhibits, and the continuity of belief and tradition that is borne out in the story of her birth and upbringing in the house of the Druid.

Her ancient origins as the goddess of poetry, smithcraft, and the hearthfire are borne out again and again in the traditions that have grown up around her and are specifically applied to her Christian form as well as to her pagan aspect. One of the most important and startling of these associations is with divination. The "Augury" or frith (pronounced "free") of Brighid grows out of the tradition that makes her the midwife and foster mother of Christ, and the perpetual helper and friend of Mary, an honor she shares with Ita of Munster. The Gaelic method of the frith was said to derive from the loss of Christ by Mary in the Temple. Brighid searches for the lost child by making a frith between her hands. This is recorded in an early text:

> The Frith That Brighid made for her Fosterling,
> Making a pipe within her palms:
> "I see my Fosterling by the well-side,
> Teaching the people without doubt.
>
> I made my frith towards the well
> And that was the best way of working:
> The King of Kings teaching the people,
> I see my Christ down there certainly."
> (trans. Caitlín Matthews)

...

This method of curling the hands to form a "seeing tube" seems originally to have been used by frithirs (pronounced "freer") for discovering lost people and animals, or to discover the health of an absent being. The use of the palms is widespread among the Irish Gaels, where the palms are used to provide a "seeing space," or tabula rasa, to block out the light or to focus the seer. The usual practice of the frith was undertaken by the frithir, fasting on the first Monday of the quarter, at sunrise, with bare head and feet. It was made in order to divine the portent for the coming quarter. Special prayers to invoke Mary and Brighid and to welcome the frith were said while walking deosil around the household fire three times. Then, with closed or blindfolded eyes, the frithir went to the threshold of the house, placing one hand on either jamb with prayers to grant the request that occasioned the frith. Then, with open eyes, she looked steadfastly ahead and noted all that she saw.

The signs are called rathadach (lucky) or rosadach (unlucky). A man or beast rising up indicates improving health, or ill health and death if lying down. A cockerel coming toward the frithir is fortunate, while other approaching birds indicate news. A duck indicates safety for sailors, while a raven indicates death.

The maintaining of the eternal flame of Kildare is central to an understanding of Brighid's place in Celtic tradition. It is more than a symbolic act, being a very profound connection to her own "fiery" nature and to the links in a chain of continuity that flow out of her dual aspected identity. A ninth-century hymn to Brighid makes a clear reference to this, as well as to the dating of her feast day, which marks the diminishing of winter and the coming of spring at the ancient Celtic festival of Imbolc on Feb 1.

I take Bride as my advocate.
Dear to me is Erin,
Dear to me each land,
Praise be to it!

O white flame of Leinster,
Enlighten the whole land,
Chief of Erin's maidens,
Chief of finest women

Dark the bitter winter,
Cutting its sharpness,
But Brighid's mantle
Brings spring to Ireland.

(trans. Caitlín Matthews)

...

Brighid's mantle (Bratach Bhrighid), also mentioned here, is continually invoked in Ireland to protect people, beasts, and houses. Midwives would leave out a special shawl on Imbolc eve so that Brighid would bless it: a shawl so blessed was considered to carry Brighid's blessing and was placed around the shoulders of laboring women to speed up their delivery.

Brighid's story is one of infinite compassion and openheartedness. She is unique among the saints in having been brought up in the house of a Druid in whose company she found it easy to be, and who himself saw and predicted much of her greatness. Her gifts are those of generosity of spirit, and whatever she touched was bound to increase. She is of primary importance in the history of the Celtic saints in that she bridges the worlds between the older traditions and the new faith, and because she represents the importance of the feminine principle for both ancient and modern. As Bride she is a goddess of profound strength, teaching the gifts of poetry and smithcraft and the importance of maintaining the fires of the hearth. As Saint Brighid she becomes a repository of the fiery light of the divine, symbolized by the perpetual flame at Kildare, which was kept alight until the dawn of the Reformation and has been rekindled by women in many parts of the world in our own time.

This symbolism of fire, which threads all through her story like a bright-gold thread, is what we may choose to remember her for today. It is the fire of inspiration, of divine insight, and of the rich heritage of the two traditions she spans. In Ireland she is still acknowledged as a patron of travelers, midwives, and healers. Her gifts in each of these areas are present in her story, which in its fullest form is an astonishing catalog of miraculous cures. The story of her presence at the birth of Christ is one of the most astonishing and connects to a number of stories in Celtic tradition that suggest that the Druids as well as others were aware of the appearance of a new aspect of universal deity.

The message that Brighid holds out to us is one of the importance of continuity, the honoring of past as well as present traditions, and the recognition that there are no breaks in the long history of spirituality. This, together with the protection she holds out to all, is borne out in a great invocation of Brighid that is found in the Hebridean tradition, which begins as follows:

> Brigit of the mantles,
> Brigit of the peats,
> Brigit of the braided hair,
> Brigit of the augury.
> (See also pp 74–75)

...

It was said that if this prayer was repeated daily, no harm would come to the person who did so. In similar fashion, recalling the eternal flames of Brighid's hearth at Kildare, Gaelic mothers would breathe these words over the fire as it was banked in for the night:

> I smoor the hearth
> As Brighid the Fostermother would smoor it.
> The holy name of the Fostermother
> Be upon the hearth and the herd,
> Be upon each of my household.
> (translated by Caitlín Matthews)

...

As she said this, she would spread the embers into a circle and divide it into three equal heaps with a central heap. To make the holy name of the foster mother, she placed three turfs of peat between the three heaps, each one touching the center, and cover all of it with ash.

Thus the protection of Brighid is wrapped about the house and its occupants, preserving the threefold integrity of the soul and enfolding it in the presence of the fires of inspiration and wholeness.

MEDITATION POINTS

- Consider what acts of compassion you have performed in your life, and what further acts you may do.

- Ask yourself what auguries you might make for your own life, and about what you would ask.

- Consider how you can increase the bounty of your spiritual life.

- Whether you are a man or a woman, consider the importance of the feminine in spiritual practice.

- Ask yourself how you can combine the inner life of the spirit with the outer life of the world.

- What kind of fire illumines your life; what inspires you and how can you find more of it in your day-to-day living?

Brighid of the mantles
(Sloinntearschid na Brighid)

Brighid, daughter of Brown Dugall,
Son of Aodh, son of Art, son of Conn,
Son of Criara, son of Cairpre, son of Cas,
Son of Cormac, son of Cartach, son of Conn.
Brighid of the mantles,
Brighid of the peats,   [turf-fuel]
Brighid of the braided hair,
Brighid of the augury.

Brighid of the shining feet,
Brighid of the quietness,
Brighid of the shining palms,
Brighid of the cattle.

Brighid, friend of women,
Brighid of the peats,
Brighid, women's midwife,
Brighid, woman of grace.

Brighid, tress of Mary,
Brighid, Foster-Mother of Christ;
Each day and each night
I say the Genealogy of Brighid:
I shall not die,
I shall not be pierced,
I shall not be imprisoned,

I shall not be ill-wished,
I shall not be riven,
I shall not be plundered,
I shall not be down-trodden,
I shall not be exposed,
I shall not be torn,
Nor will Christ
Be forgetful of me.

No sun shall burn me,
No fire shall scorch me,
No beam shall pierce me,
No moon shall blanch me.

No waters shall drown me,
No brine shall choke me,
No flood overwhelm me,
No stream shall drown me.
No vexatious word shall quell me,
No black slumber shall oppress me,
No drunken stupor fall upon me,
No quicken-ash spell lie upon me.

I am under the protection
Of Holy Mary;
And my dear companion
Is Brighid.

(Translated by Caitlín Matthews)

...

FOUR

THE WISDOM OF WILD WORDS

COLUMBA OF IONA
(June 9)

Behold Iona!
A blessing on every eye that see it!
He who does good for another here,
Will be repaid a thousandfold!
(Attributed to Colmcille)

...

Columba, or as he is more properly called, Colmcille, is rightly deemed one of the greatest of the Celtic saints. His wisdom, recorded sometimes in his own words, is warm and joyful, and the events of his life are as remarkable as any of those who appear in this book. Indeed, there is so much that one might gainfully learn from his life that it was difficult to know what to put in and what to leave out.

Born at Gartan, a wild district in Donegal, on December 7, 521, of royal stock, Colmcille was educated by the great Finian of Clonrad, who also had Ciaran as a pupil (see chapter 10). Between 546 and 599 he founded a number of important monasteries, including those at Derry, Durrow, and Kells. In 580 he took part in an assembly at Druim-Cetta, where he argued in favor of the Bardic community of Ireland and was thus largely responsible for saving them from extinction.

But most famously, he is known as the founder of a community on the tiny island of Iona in 563, where he settled after being driven into exile—why is not known—from Ireland. He remained there for the rest of his days, making only occasional forays into Ireland, where he kept a kind of overlordship from afar. From the tiny island southwest of Scotland, given to him by the king of the Irish, Dalraida, Colmcille radiated wisdom and strength of purpose. He is known as a fine poet and a brilliant scholar, and several surviving works are attributed to him, though none with certainty. His biographer, Adomnan, describes him vividly as tall, powerfully built, and possessed of a commanding presence. Just but never overly harsh, he gave himself single-handily to the creation of the foundations of wisdom for which he is famed. His whole life was dedicated by learning, and a passion for the truth that shines forth in every line of his life. He saw the need for education among the people whose spiritual lives he oversaw, and he dedicated much of his life to the furtherance of the skills of reading and writing. He was also a visionary whose prophecies are an astonishing catalog of events that have an important bearing on the inner history of the Celts in Ireland.

Whatever the reason for his exile, it obviously meant a great deal to Colmcille. A poem attributed to him puts these feelings across in words drenched with the pain of homesickness:

> How delightful it would be,
> O son of Mary,
> To cross the sea,
> The well of floods,
> To Ireland.
>
> To Mag nEolairg by Benevanagh,
> Across Loch Foyle where
> The harmony of swans
> Would offer comfort to me . . .
>
> To listen early in Ross Grencha
> To the call of the stags;
> To hear the cuckoos calling
> From the brink of the summer woods.
>
> I have left three things
> I Loved the best:
> Durrow, Derry, and Tir Luigdech—
> I have loved the lands of Ireland.
>
> •••

This is the voice of a man who loved the world as much as he loved the places of the soul; whose long and sometimes difficult journey never ceased to burn with the light of inspiration and a deep love for all created things.

Decades before his birth, Columba's coming was predicted. First by a wise man named Maucta, who said, "In the last ages of the world [as it was deemed in those days] a son shall be born who shall be called Columba, and whose name shall be known in every corner of these islands. Bright as a star shall he shine, and all men shall recognize his wisdom."

Long after this, in the time of Conall Gulban, son of the great hero Niall of the Nine Hostages, it happened that Conall was hunting one day near Gartan in the province of Derry. And though his hounds several times raised and cornered game, each time they turned away and would not kill it. Conall marveled greatly at this and, upon returning home, consulted his Druids concerning it. They told him that a child would be born to the third generation hence of his line, and that it would be a marvelous child, and because it was to be born in that place where he had been hunting, so the hounds had spared the game in token of the future peacemaker whose name would be Columba.

These things were recorded in the books of the wise, and when Columba was born, many recalled them and knew that a rare being had come into the world.

Fedlimid (son of Fergus, son of Conall Bulban, son of Niall of the Nine Hostages) and Ethne (the daughter of Dima, who was descended from Cathair the Great) were his parents. While she was great with child, Ethne had a dream in which she was given a great cloak. So vast was this garment that it stretched over much of Ireland and Scotland, as well as the seas between, and it was made up of every color imaginable, woven in shifting patterns of light. In her dream, a youth of radiant beauty came and took the cloak from her, and this made Ethne sad. But the youth spoke to her and gave her comfort. "Lady," he said, "you have no need of sorrow, for the meaning of this cloak is that your son, who shall be born into the world soon, shall send forth his light over Ireland and Scotland, and everyone shall acknowledge the wisdom of his words." And as Ethne awoke, she seemed to hear the voice of the youth bidding her to name her child "Columba," which means "dove" in the Celtic tongue.

Soon after that, Ethne's time came upon her, and it is said that she went forth into the wilderness and brought forth her child alone and unaided. Some say also that she brought forth a red stone at that time, and that in after years it was seen to perform miracles of healing. But whether this is true or not, there was no doubting that the child was marked out from the beginning to be special.

In accordance with the custom of the time, he was given into the care of fosterage. The one chosen for this task was named Cruithnechan, a wise and generous man who was skilled in learning. From the start, he declared the child to be quick and adept at all things, and that he displayed a wisdom far beyond his years. One night, coming home late, Cruithnechan saw the sleeping Columba surrounded by light of such brilliance that he could scarcely bear to look upon it. From this, as from other signs, he knew that the boy was filled with a special power, and to Ethne and Fedlimid he declared his intention of placing him in the care of the wise and noble Finian, who was a tutor to many of the greatest of the Celli Dé.

Soon after this, as he lay abed, it seemed to Columba that a shining being came to him and wished him well. "Who are you?" asked Columba. "I am your guardian," answered the Shining One. "Wherever you go, I shall walk with you and be your guide." Columba's eyes opened wide. "What is your name?" he asked. "You may called me Axal, which means 'helper,'" answered the Shining One. And thus it was that even before he had entered upon the course of his life, Columba learned that he was to be guided and protected in all that he did.

Columba at Clonard

So Columba went to Clonard and was welcomed by Finian, who already knew that he was to be a remarkable pupil. Indeed, it was at this time that Finian had the vision in which he saw the moon and the sun rise in the sky at the same time, and the moon went and stood over the northern part of Ireland and over Scotland, while the sun went and stood over the center of Ireland. And as has been told elsewhere (see chapter 10), the significance of this sign was that the moon stood for Columba and the sun for Ciaran and for the great deeds they would do in these lands.

Now, it was the custom that each new pupil at Clonard should build his own hut in which he would live while he was there. Columba asked Finian where he should build his. "Put it by the door of the church," replied Finian, "for I see that you shall yourself be a doorway to many." But when Columba built his bothy, it was not outside the door of the church but some ways to the left, and only in years later was the building extended in such a way that the door stood precisely where Columba had lived. It may well be that this was the first real sign of the prophetic ability that Columba was to display so markedly in his life.

Columba remained at Clonard for a time and learned much wisdom from Finian and enjoyed the company of his other pupils, including Ciaran, who became his soul friend thereafter, and with others who were to establish many great houses of wisdom in Ireland.

When Columba had been at Clonard only a few years, it is told that a plague came upon the land, and that Finian sent his pupils way to ensure their safety, though he himself would not leave. Columba went on his way to his home at Gartan, and when he reached the stream known as the Bir, he blessed its waters. The plague continued to spread through the land unchecked until it came to the banks of the Bir, and there it stopped and came no farther because of the power of Columba.

Columba in the Oak Groves

Soon after came word of the death of Finian, and Columba mourned his old friend and teacher greatly. Yet, he also said, "This is the sign that I have awaited. For now, I must go and teach the ways of God throughout Ireland." And thus he began to follow the wandering way, traveling to every part of the land and sharing his learning and wisdom with all who would listen. In time he came to the place called Derry, and there he founded his first great school. Ever after he spoke of this place as especially dear to him, for it was possessed of the oak knowledge of an older time (indeed, the name "Derry" comes from the word for oak in the tongue of Ireland). Of this place Columba was to write:

For this reason do I love Derry:
For the smoothness of its hills,
for purity of its airs,
And because it is filled with shining angels
From one end to the other.

...

But the first days in that place were not easy for Columba and his followers. For when he ordered some trees to be felled to begin building the monastery, a certain warrior on whose lands they were became angry that Columba had not asked his consent before beginning the work. When he heard this, Columba said, "Tare the worth of the wood in barley grain and tell the warrior to plant it at once." Now it was close to midsummer at the time, long past the time for planting. But though the lord scorned the offering, yet he planted it, and it grew and was ripe in time for harvest nonetheless, so that thereafter the warrior troubled Columba and his followers no more.

So for a time, Columba continued to travel about Ireland, until it chanced that he angered one of the kings of that land who ordered him sent into exile. Many said that he should stay, but rather than cause trouble in his beloved land, Columba chose to depart. "It seems to me," he said, "that another place awaits me." And with a small company of his closest followers, he set sail forthwith for the land of Scotland. But before he was to set foot upon that shore, his ship was drawn away by tide and current until it landed upon an island called Hy. Today this place is known as Iona and is regarded as sacred by all who set foot upon its soil. Here Columba knew that he had found a place that would be home for him thereafter. And so he set about building a place of shelter where all who wished might come to learn and share the wisdom he himself had begun to discover. But as fast as they built, in the night there came a force that threw down all they had accomplished. At last, one of his companions, a man named Odran, came forward and said, "Master, a vision has been granted to me. A deep disturbance is under the earth, and one of us must go there living before our foundations will stand. I wish it to be me." At first, Columba would hear nothing of this, for it seemed to him a dark thing to do. But when two more nights passed and the work of the brothers was thrown down, he saw the truth of Odran's words. With much ceremony, the brother was interred alive close to the center of the island, and from that night the foundations of the building remained untouched. But Columba could not rest. Every morning for the next five days, he walked to the site of Odran's grave and returned full of sorrow. At length he could bear it no longer. "I must look one more time upon the face of Odran," he said. And so the brethren returned to the place where they had buried their companion and began to dig.

Soon they uncovered the simple coffin in which Odran had been interred. Columba himself opened the lid, and then it was that there occurred a strange and wonderous thing. For Odran opened his eyes and sat up! He looked at the brothers and into the eyes of Columba and spoke.

> *I have been where no living man has been,*
> *And I must speak.*
> *Heaven is not as we think,*
> *Nor is Hell as we think;*
> *Nor are the good eternally happy,*
> *Nor the bad eternally sorrowful . . .*
>
> ...

He would have spoken more, but Columba held up his hand and ordered the brothers to depart. And indeed, they were glad enough to leave, for they were fearful at Odran's words. But Columba remained there at the gravesite for some time. After, when he came away, the earth was back upon the tomb of Odran, and Columba never spoke of what he had heard. Ever after, the place was known as Relig Odran, "the grave of Odran," and all the brethren of the community who died were buried there.

After this the community grew apace, and though he traveled far afield in the years to come, Columba always returned to Iona, and because of him the island became a shining light for all the world. But though he learned to love the bright sky arching above the green earth and the bare rocks, Columba's heart ever yearned for the shores of Ireland, and in more than one poem that he wrote, he expressed the deep yearning of his soul for his homeland.

Columba's Prophecies

Every day Columba used to have one of his followers give as much food as he could spare to the poor, and every day many came to receive his gifts. But one day a man came after all the rest, and the brother whose task it was to give out the alms turned him away and told him to come again next day. On the morrow the same man came again, but once again he was too late, and again the almoner turned him away. Then the man looked at the brother and said, "Go and tell Columba that he has more than enough to feed as many as will come here, and that he shall offer more than food for the body."

When he heard this, Columba jumped up and ran after the man without waiting to put on either his cloak or his shoes. When he overtook him, the two fell in beside each other and spoke together for a time. But soon the man who had come begging vanished away, and Columba returned home alone and silent. But from that day forward he was possessed of a gift that was both a blessing and a terror—the gift of inner sight, which caused him to see things that had yet to be or that took place far away. Again and again he would stop whatever he was doing and laugh or smile or weep, according to what he saw with his inner sight. Once, standing in the midst of a field of scarlet poppies, he said, "Ah, Bishop Colman has just left Ireland to come to us. He is facing a dreadful storm at Brecken's whirlpool. Even now he raises his hands to heaven to ask that his ship be spared. Let us all join with him in wishing him a safe and speedy passage." And, sure enough, in a matter of days the good Colman arrived and told of his journey, and it was just as Columba had said.

Another time he was with King Aidan of the Southern Cruitne, and the king asked him which of his three eldest sons would rule after him. "None of them," said Columba, "for all three shall be killed in battle. Rather it is one of your younger sons who shall follow you." Then he bade the king call the youths to come to him. And Columba said, "Whichever one of them comes to me and lays his head upon my breast, he shall be king after you." And when the three youths entered the room, one of them, who was named Eochid Buide, came and laid his head on Columba's breast. Columba blessed him, and afterward it was just as he had prophesied, for the three elder sons were slain at the battle of Miathi, and of his remaining sons, all perished save Eochid, who thus followed his father as king of that place.

As time passed, it seemed that Columba could see beyond the bounds of the present with increasing ease, and that all things were transparent to him. Again and again he foretold events that were to come, and things ever fell out as he had said. On one occasion a man named Colic, who would come to hold high office in the ranks of the Celli Dé, asked to know the manner of his death. Columba shut his eyes tightly and said, "You shall live a long life, Colic, but when one day you see your cook making merry with his kin of an evening, you shall know that your time is soon to come." And thus it came about, just as Columba had seen.

His prophecies were not always of such high matters. One day as he was sitting in the scriptorium, preparing the lettering of a great page, he suddenly stopped and frowned. His attendant, Diormit, seeing this, asked what was amiss. "Truly, it is nothing," replied Columba. "Only that a man who is at present on the other side of the island, but who will join us later, shall knock over my inkpot and cause me to do this page again." And so it came about, for Diormit watched and sure enough a guest came that night who, while looking at the work of the brothers in the scriptorium, spilled ink on the page that Columba himself had been lettering, so that it must be done again.

On another occasion, Columba called one of the brothers to him and said, "On the third day from now you must go to the western side of the island, to the shore. There you will find a crane that has journeyed from a distant land and, having suffered much from contrary winds, will be utterly spent. Take care of the bird and see that it is fed and looked after." The brother did as he had been told, and sure enough he found the crane just as Columba had said, and cared for it for three days until it was strong enough to continue on its way. When he returned to the foundation, Columba smiled upon him and, without waiting for him to relate any of what had occurred, thanked him for caring for "the stranger from a foreign land."

Many said that Columba knew of these things from the Shining One named Axal, who always went with him and with whom he spoke often of deep matters; but others believed that Columba had the ability to look into the Inner Place and of seeing what was there, just as the Druids did. Whatever the truth of the matter, throughout his long life Columba made many such prophecies, and many of these were written down and collected in a great book. And in time, all of them came to pass as Columba had foretold.

Columba and Mongan

There came a time when Columba could no longer bear to be parted from his own country, and he therefore journeyed into Ireland. Once there, he made his way to Carraic Eolaire, on the banks of Loch Foyle, which was a solitary spot such as he might use to contemplate and enjoy his homeland in comfort. Less than an hour had he been there when there came toward him across the water a youth of exceeding beauty, who walked on sandals of bronze upon the water as though it were the earth.

"May the gods of worship bless you, Columba," said the youth.

"Who are you that greets me thus?" demanded Columba.

"Mongan mac Fiachna is my name. I am the son of the king of Ulster."

"How is it that you are alone if you are truly a king's son?" asked Columba.

"As to that, you are alone, are you not?" replied the youth. "Be assured that I could have twice ten thousand men at my side in an instant if I so desired."

"Then why have you come here?" said Columba.

"I have heard that you are great in wisdom," said Mongan. "And, since I am reckoned wise among my people, I have come to match wits with you."

Columba smiled. "Tell me something of this great knowledge and wisdom that you have," he said.

"Ah," said Mongan. "There is not a creature in all of the world, from the smallest gnat to the greatest whale, whose shape I cannot put upon me. Also, I have knowledge of the hidden isles to the west, where few have ever been from the world of men."

"Then tell me," said Columba. "Who dwells in these hidden isles?"

"A fair company indeed," replied Mongan. "They have upon them the shape of the fairest men and women, and they possess a great many cattle and sheep; the cattle white as foam, save that their ears are red, and the sheep also white, and more of them there are than the stars in the sky."

"This sounds a most wondrous place," replied Columba. "But tell me what knowledge you have of heaven?"

"I know nothing of this place save for rumors," replied Mongan cautiously. "Will you show me something of it?"

"Return here tomorrow and I shall show you indeed," said Columba.

With that, the beautiful youth vanished away and Columba fell to contemplation and prayer.

Next day, Mongan came once again walking across the waters of the loch.

"Well," he said, "I am come. What wonders will you show me?"

Columba smiled. "Put your head under the corner of my mantle," he said, "and you shall see all that you would see."

Without hesitation, Mongan did as he was bidden, and for a time there was silence, save only for the song of birds and the lap of water.

After a time, Columba lifted the edge of his cloak, revealing the face of Mongan, whose eyes were closed in sleep. A smile was on his face, and when Columba woke him gently, he sprang up and said, "I have seen such things as no tongue could ever tell. Truly this heaven of your is a most wondrous place. And, most strange of all, it is very like the Otherworld to which I have often journeyed. And yet . . ."

"The same, but different?" asked Columba.

Mongan nodded.

"Then here is a mystery we must both contemplate," said Columba. And with that, they took leave of each other, and soon after Columba returned to Iona. But he never forgot their meeting by Loch Foyle and in later years often spoke of the mystery of the place that was akin to heaven.

The Quest for the Wisdom of the Past

This was not the only time that Columba encountered the ancient wisdom of Ireland. There was at a certain time a gathering of bards at the court of the king of Connecht. Senchan, the high bard of Erin, was their leader, and he demanded the right of all bards to be served and honored by the king on pain of satire—for it is well known in those times that if a bard made a satire of any man or woman living, they would suffer greatly because of it. After a time, the king grew tired of feeding this company, who numbered more than three hundred men, women, and servants. Therefore, he asked them to move on to another place. At this, Senchan grew enraged and laid a curse upon all of Connacht, that no poem or bardic song should be heard in that court until they had discovered all the great epics concurring the Cattle Raid of Challenge, which in that time had been forgotten and had not been recited in all of Ireland for many years.

The king of Connacht was greatly disturbed by this, for though he loved to hear the entertainments of the bards, in no wise did he know how he might discover the lost epic. Then his brother Marban came to him and said, "Go and seek Columba, for there is no wisdom and knowledge that is not known to him."

So the king, hearing that Columba was in Ireland, went and sought him out. When he heard of the difficulty the king was suffering, Columba thought deeply upon the matter and spoke with the Shining One, who went with him always. Then he spoke with the king and said that the only way that he would discover the words of the forgotten epic were to go to the tomb of the mighty hero Fergus mac Roich, for whom the raid of which the poem dealt had been carried out, more than a thousand years before.

So it was that Columba and many of his fellows, together with the king of Connacht, went to the place where Fergus was buried, and there Columba and his brethren, many of whom were holy men and leaders in their own right, prayed and meditated for a day and a night. At the end of that time, Fergus appeared before them from the Land of Wonder. So mighty and tall was he that he needed to bend down and lie full length upon the earth before he could be heard. Then Columba begged him to help the king of Connacht by telling him the story of the Cattle Raid, and because of the love that he felt for his descendants in the land of Ireland, Fergus recited the whole of the epic, which was written down on the hide of a famous dun cow, for which reason ever after this writing was known as "The Book of the Dun Cow," which may still be read to this day. Then Columba thanked the spirit of Fergus and bade him return to the Land of Wonder. The king in turn thanked Columba and returned with the book to Connacht and summoned Senchan so that he might hear it recited. And when the chief poet did so, he was filled with wonder at the power of Columba.

The White Horse

Now, Columba had always known when his death would come, and there came a day, when he was advanced in years and worn out with traveling and teaching, that it was time for him to depart this life. So he set forth for one last time to travel across the island and visit with those of his brethren who had established small enclaves of their own. As he went, Columba grew tired and sat down by the side of the road to rest. As he remained there, a white horse appeared before him and came and laid its head on his feet. Afterward, Columba's attendants said that they saw tears gather in its eyes and roll down its cheeks. But Columba stroked its muzzle and bade it not to grieve just as it had been a man. Soon the beast rose to its feet, but still it stood by, offering to carry the old man on its back. Columba, however, shook his head. "I have waked thus far through the world and I have not much farther to go," he said. "But I thank you nonetheless." At these words the white horse was gone from there as suddenly as it had come, and all marveled thereat, knowing that such a creature was of the Otherworld and reckoned sacred. But Columba merely smiled and said that he had many friends.

Death and the Calming of the Sea

So at length, Columba returned from his circuit of the island. He stood for a time on the hill overlooking the foundation where he had lived and taught for so many years, and raised his hands in blessing. Then he went down to the scriptorium, where he had spent many hours, and continued working on the page of the Gospels that he had been illuminating. As evening drew in, he said, "After this page, Baithene must continue the work." Soon after, he laid down his stylus and, with a sigh, made his way to his room. When the bell rang for the midnight service, Columba arose and made his way to the chapel, and several who saw him said that he was running as though he were a youth of twenty years or less. Once there, he fell upon the ground. There his attendant Diormit found him and cradled him in his arms. Columba looked up at the brethren who gathered about him, and smiled upon them all. Then he gave up the ghost.

Two days later he was interred with due solemnity in the graveyard close to the monastery, that same graveyard that housed the bones of Odran. It is told that a great storm arose on the day of Columba's death, but that at the moment he was laid to rest, it ceased and the waters became calm again. Many came from all parts of the land to honor his passing. Later on, his body would be removed from its resting place and reinterred in a grave adjacent to that in which his great soul friends Patrick and Brighid lay. Columba himself had foreseen this, as did others possessed of foresight. The great poet Dallan Forgail, who knew Columba for a friend to all who sought after knowledge, wrote of him, later:

Noble the tide that reached Iona
For he that shall be twice buried,
Columba, true and pure,
Son of the king of Heaven and Earth.

Iona of many saints
Foundation of Columba the mighty
Therefrom at length he departed
To his joyous bright dwelling.

...

Thus may Columba be remembered!

Columba's story is largely concerned with vision and the intermingling of this world with the other. Again and again we read of the saint's ability to foretell the future, as when he prophesies the fate of the king of Southern Cruitne's sons or seems aware of the difficulties being experienced by a visiting bishop at that moment many miles away.

Celtic tradition is full of seers and prophets, and it is very easy to see how the life of Columba has inherited something of the style and content of prophetic abilities of such figures as the Welsh Taliesin and Merlin and the Irish Fionn and Amairgin. In most cases where these figures are present, the connection is made among wisdom, knowledge, and vision, all of which Columba manifested in his own life, while in the lore of the Druids we find these gifts divided up into three orders: the bards, who stored up knowledge; the Druids themselves, who taught the knowledge; and the ovates or seers, who journeyed into the inner places of the soul to bring back the accumulated wisdom of the ancestors.

It is not really surprising that we find a huge catalog of prophetic utterances attributed to Columba that rival those of Merlin. The only surprising thing is that the subject of these stories is a Christian saint and that there is no real emphasis on God as the source of this wisdom. Rather, Columba seems to possess one of the type of figures generally referred to as a "spirit ally" or "inner guide," to which there are many references in Celtic tradition. Such figures are not unlike the invisible friends often described by children. Attributed more often than not to "an overactive imagination," such figures may be very real and may well have provided us with the concept of the guardian angel.

The actual source of Columba's visionary abilities can be traced to two significant points in his life. The first is to the appearance of the mysterious being who calls himself Axal, "Helper." He is generally supposed to have been an angel, though even Columba's biographers seem hesitant to say this with absolute certainty. This is certainly the only example of a Celtic saint whose inner guide is named, though as we have seen, many of those who appear in this book had similar inner helpers to whom they could turn in times of need. Columba seems to have been particularly sensitive to such inner prompting, and the examples of his insight and prophetic gifts are cataloged extensively in all the versions of his life.

The second point from which his prophetic skills seem to derive is the meeting with the mysterious beggar who always comes late. One text suggests that the visitor was none other than Christ, though this is probably a late insertion. The truth is that like many wise and holy men, this is a turning point in Columba's life—and as with so many other such people, once the stranger comes, nothing is ever the same after.

But the gift is a two-edged sword, for those who have the sight do not always see what they wish to see and have no control over the way they use it. To see terrible things that will happen to others is no easy matter and requires sensitive handling. Many who are offered this gift turn away from it, fearing to see things that they cannot bear to relate. This is the eternal problem of the seer, and only time and belief in the essential goodness of the gift can bring them to a full understanding of it. Used wisely, it can heal and redirect us on our spiritual path; used unwisely, it can break the bonds of friendship, love, and trust.

Two of the most extraordinary events in Columba's life are the episode of the burial of Odran and the appeal to the spirit of Fergus Mac Roith concerning the lost epic poem of the cattle raid. The first episode, which is significantly expunged from most of the versions of the life, has so many echoes of ancient Celtic traditions as to be truly unique. In the first place, there is a marked similarity with the story of Merlin, the famous seer of King Arthur's court, who in an early episode is to be offered as a child sacrifice to enable a building to be completed—a building that, like the one in the story of Columba, falls down mysteriously every night. Merlin avoids this fate by giving vent to prophetic utterance, rather as Odran does. However, while Merlin's prophecies are gathered and recorded, Odran's are not. The reason being, as we are led to understand in the life of Columba, because his references to heaven, being not what we expect, might be threatening to the faith of those who expected to go there. In the original version of the story, no sooner has Odran begun to speak than Columba cried, "Earth, Earth upon Odran!," causing him to be immured again at once. I have suggested that Columba's innate curiosity as a scholar might have led him to listen to more of what Odran had to say (at least in private), as is suggested by his encounter with the mysterious figure of Mongan, who, despite describing himself merely as "the king of Ulster's son," is well known in Celtic mythology as an otherworldly personage. The exchange between Mongan and Columba is a testament both to the latter's curiosity and to the evident parallels between the Christian heaven and the Celtic otherworld, while the placing of Odran in the darkness under the earth is a well-known method of calling forth a vision as described in more-ancient Celtic traditions.

When it comes to the need for information relating to the wisdom of such ancient times, Columba does not hesitate to assemble his followers and to pray over the tomb of the pagan hero Fergus Mac Roith, in order to call him back from the Land of Wonder and to take down the information he has to give. The entire book-length poem is dictated to the saint and is written down on parchment made from the skin of his favorite dun cow. This became "The Book of the Dun Cow," which still exists today, while the poem, known as "The Tain," is perhaps the most famous epic text to have come out of the ancient Celtic past.

The point here is not only that the saints asked an older figure for information, but that Columba received it through prayer and vision and recorded it on the skin of cow—recalling an ancient shamanic method of receiving visions by wrapping oneself in the hide of a yellow cow or a sacred bull before "dreaming" the answer to specific questions. Such practices, like so many of those attributed to the Celtic saints, are very closely allied to those of the worldwide discipline of shamanism. Indeed, as noted elsewhere throughout his book, the notion that the saints were "Christian shamans" is a very real possibility.

Much of the underlying power of Columba's story comes from a very human need to know something of the future, to peer beyond the veil and catch a glimpse of what will come to pass. The ability to do this comes not only from a deep awareness of the spiritual worlds, but also from a close observance and attunement to the rhythms of life itself. Most people will have been aware at some time or other in their life journey of a sense of predestination. This is not to say that our freedom to choose is taken from us, but rather that certain patterns exist that indicate the connectedness of all things.

This idea is inherent in the majority of the lives of the Celtic saints and, like many of their teachings, is in part an inheritance of more-ancient beliefs. Our own sense of such a relationship with the cosmos may come only in flashes, but it is possible to extend this for longer periods. Those with such abilities are called prophets and visionaries, people who are so deeply connected to the immense mystery of the universe that they can, quite literally, see through it into the future and into other times and places.

Columba's ability to do this was well attested, and our own latent ability to achieve a similar state of being is by no means impossible. Daily meditation on the small and particular connections—which we often call coincidence or synchronicity—between one event and another can gradually open our awareness to the larger patterns that are wound into and through the shape of our spiritual journey. This kind of awareness, which is akin to the Tibetan notion of "mindfulness," is not something to be feared but rather embraced. It teaches us how to be "daily visionaries," to perceive the patterns that shape our lives and to become aware of the many kinds of reciprocity that are an everyday aspect of living.

MEDITATION POINTS

- What patterns can you perceive in your daily life?

- Are there any larger patterns in your life as a whole?

- Consider if you have ever experienced anything like a flash of future vision.

- Ask yourself how this might have come about and whether it subsequently came true.

- Draw a "map" of your spiritual journey, showing how certain key points are connected.

- Meditate on this and try to see the "hidden" aspects of which you are currently unaware.

- Consider any inner connections of which you are aware in your daily life and that of the world.

Columba's Song of his Exile

Swiftly speeds my coracle,
Its stern toward Derry;
Despite deep grief,
I set my face toward Alba.[Scotland]

My coracle sings to the waves,
Yet, my eyes fill with tears;
Though God blows me East,
My heart yearns for the West.

Never more shall my eyes
Feast upon Erin's shores;
Never more shall my ears
Hear her children's song.

Hard-hearted folk in Alba
Jealous and harsh,
Their bodies ill-clothed,
Wracked with disease.

In Eire all hearts are soft,
Tempers gentler, kindly;
The women fair and wise,
The men strong and sturdy.

Trees bent double with fruit;
Bushes full of blue sloes,
Plains lush with grass,
Cattle healthy and fat.

Sweet songs the holy brothers sing
And birds chant with them;
The young are courteous,
The old full of wisdom's words.

My heart's full of love
For my glorious land;
If death should take me
I would grieve the most for Erin's fields.

If Alba were all mine,
From the center to the shore,
I would gladly exchange it
For a field in Durrow or Derry.

Westward take my blessing,
To Eire let my love fly home;
Yet carry my hope Eastward
To Alba's shining shore.

(Translated by J.M.)

...

FIVE

THE FRIEND OF ANGELS

SENAN OF SCATTERY
(March 8)

Excellent moon, brilliant as the day!
Above the plain he illumines
The tribes of Ireland;
With his many-ranked followers
He sailed through the high heavens.
—*Amra Senain*

•••

Like with Berach (chapter 12), little is known with any certainty about Senan. His name means "Old Bright One," which has led to a suggestion that he might have inherited something of the nature and qualities of an old lunar deity. A poem, the "Amra Senain," attributed to the poet Dallan Forgail, compares him to the moon, his followers to stars, and his work to a river flowing through Ireland. His name appears in several of the oldest genealogies, and he seems to have been a nobleman, despite the fact that the Life refers to him as the son of a farmer. Born near Kilrush in County Clare, he studied first with Cassidan at Irrus, then with the famous Nótal at Kilkenny. He is credited with founding several monastic settlements, including one at Inniscarra near Cork, Inis Mor, Mutton Island, and Scattery Island, which was probably the most famous. Ruins can still be seen there today, though they are probably later than the sixth century, when Senan was active. His bell (actually a small reliquary) is to be found in the museum of the Royal Irish Academy.

Senan's life paints a picture of a somewhat reluctant leader, who nonetheless was possessed of considerable powers—including him bringing back to life a chieftain's son, and the banishment of a monster inhabiting the islands where he wished to build. He seems to have been constantly befriended by angels, as witnessed by the episode of the mysterious helper at the mill (see below) and the advice he seems able to claim at almost any time. He stood always on the edge of the realm of the spirit, moving easily between states of being, which ranged from the heights of spiritual insight to the daily work of herding cattle and milling corn. Where these two worlds mingled, the wonder, and the miracles, took place.

One time when Patrick was in Domnach Mor, a deputation came from the people of Corco-Baiscinn to ask that he visit them and give them the gift of blessing. And Patrick, whose great strength was waning at that time, told them he was too weary to travel to Corco-Baiscinn, which lay across a wide expanse of sea from Domnach Mor. Next day, they came to him again and again begged him to accompany them. But Patrick would not go, for he had looked into the innermost place of his soul and seen that another would come who would do that work of blessing for him. First, he said to them, "Is your land visible from any part of this land?" "Indeed it is," said they. "From the hill named Findine, you may see part of our land."

"Then let us go there," said Patrick.

So they went to the hill of Findine, and from there Patrick blessed the land of the Corco-Baiscinn with increase and well-being throughout the times to come. And he said to them, "There is no need for me to go into your land. For there is even now a child in the womb of a woman of your people that shall do my work for me and bring blessing upon all who seek it and honor to you all."

At this, the people of Corco-Baiscinn were amazed, and they were content with what they had been told. Then Patrick pointed to an island that lay in the sea between the two lands. "What place is that?" he asked. "That is the island of Inis Cathaig," said they. "Who dwells there?" asked Patrick. "No one," said they, "for it is inhabited by a monster that allows no man to come ashore and live."

"This creature does but the work of God," said Patrick, "for it maintains the island that shall one day become a center of wisdom. And the child of whom I have spoken shall come there and build a great foundation and rule over it."

Then he blessed them all again and sent them on their way.

First Wonders

Not long after this, there was a great assembly and feasting among the people of Corco-Baiscinn, and there among those gathered were a farmer named Gerrgenn and his wife, Coimgell. When they came into the hall, a certain Druid, who was greatly respected, rose to his feet and honored these two. Everyone there was greatly astonished at this, for though the couple were well enough liked, they were not greatly born or rich. But when they asked the Druid why he honored them, he said, "It is not the man or the woman I honor but the child in the woman's womb. For vision has told me that he shall be called great and wise and that his coming has been foretold." Then the people remembered Patrick's words and marveled greatly thereat.

Soon after, Coimgell gave birth to a son, whom they named Senan, which means "the Old Bright One" in the ancient tongue of Ireland. a strange name many thought this to be, but there were others who murmured that this was not the first time that the soul within the child had walked on the earth. The woman was alone when the pains of birth came upon her, walking in the garden. But it is said that one of the Shining Ones attended upon her and eased her pain. And it is told also that the rowan stake that she held in her hands while giving birth took root and burst into flower. Some say that it may still be seen there, in the place called Magh Lacha.

Not long after the birth of her son, Coimgell went to the well to fetch water, carrying the child with her at her bosom. Near the well side grew a bush filled with ripe blackberries, and there the woman tarried for a while, stripping the fruit from a branch. After a time, she heard the voice of the child speaking within her mind: "This is rich fruit, Mother, but there is a richer kind grows on the borderlands of the spirit." Then she knew indeed that Patrick's words of a wondrous child referred to her own son.

The Fire That Did Not Burn

When Senan was but a youth, the Corco-Baiscinn went on a hosting into the lands of Corcomumruad. Senan was forced to go with them according to the laws of the time, but he had no heart in him to join in the battle or follow the warrior's way. Therefore, as the host of the Corco-Baiscinn set forth to ravage the land of their weaker neighbors, Senan went into a barn and lay down to sleep. All around on every side, the land was ravaged but the barn was spared, being somehow unseen by the host. Thus when the warriors returned to their own land, they left Senan behind, still sleeping. When the folk returned to their burned and blighted homes, they found the barn standing, though it seemed to them that flames encircled it and rose above its roof without consuming so much as a single plank of wood or blade of corn.

In time, the flames, if such they were, receded and the people were able to enter the barn. There they found Senan sleeping and would have slain him. But something held their hands, and instead they awoke him and asked when he came. In shame, Senan confessed that he had come with the host of Corco-Baiscinn, but that he had taken no part in the ravaging. Then some were mindful to kill Senan outright, but others pointed out that not only had the barn been saved by his presence, but the land in the immediate area had also escaped the ravages of the host, while others spoke of the strange fire that burned without consuming. So in the end, Senan's life was spared and he returned home unscathed.

The Road of the Oxen

One day, Senan was herding his father's oxen. He was to drive them from Irrus, where they were gathered, to Magh Lacha, and between those places there was an arm of the sea that rose in tumult at certain tides. When Senan arrived at the crossing place, the waters were already high and darkness was beginning to fall. Senan went to the fortress of Mechair, which overlooked the estuary, and begged for shelter for himself and the oxen. But Mechair was away, and his servants would not admit anyone. So Senan went back to the edge of the sea and stood there for a long while, while the cold bit deeper into his bones.

Then he said, "Enough is enough. I am done with this work." And he raised his hand over the water, which retreated before him and gave way so that he might drive the oxen across in safety. So then Senan went home and told his father that he intended to go to study with the wise and holy teacher Notal, at his school in Cell Manach in the district of Ossory.

Next day, Senan set out for Cell Manach and was made welcome. He discovered that his first task was herding the cattle belonging to the foundation, and this he ruefully accepted. But when it came to the time when he must separate the calves from the cattle, he found that whenever he set the calves upon one side, the cows would at once go there, and when he drove the cows away, the calves followed them. In exasperation, Senan drew a line in the earth and blessed it, and thereafter the cows and cattle went on either side of the line and made no move to cross it. When he saw this, Notal smiled and remembered Patrick's words concerning Senan and knew that a rare, wondrous being had entered the fold of his flock.

The Wondrous Miller

Another of Senan's tasks was to mill corn for the household, and this he loved to do. But one time there was widespread famine in the area, and two robbers were abroad who sought to steal anything they could and sell it for profit. Hearing that the mill of Cell Manach was still active and had grain to spare, they went there at night, expecting to find only a lone man whom they could easily overpower. When they looked through a crack in the door, however, they saw two people, one operating the mill while the other read from a book.

The two men took thought about this and decided to wait until morning. "For," said they, "surely one of these men will come forth and go to his home, and when he does so, we can ambush him and take the corn he has ground." So they watched all night, and when they looked through the crack in the wall, they saw that one of the two men had fallen asleep, but the other toiled on ceaselessly until morning.

When day broke, the youth who had been reading came forth with a bag of grain over his shoulder. The two men sprang out and looked into the mill, which was empty. "Where is the fellow who was helping you all last night?" they demanded. Senan, for it was he indeed, looked at them and smiled. "There was no man there but myself," he answered.

"But we saw another," the robbers said.

"I said no 'man,'" replied Senan with a smile. For a moment the two felt the presence of another just behind the youth, and such wonder overcame them that they cast themselves at his feet and begged his forgiveness and blessing. Later they became Senan's devoted followers when he gathered others about him to hear his teachings and learn from his shining example. It was they who told this story long after, and all knew then that it was one of the Shining Ones who had helped Senan in the mill, for others afterward spoke of the youth who worked alone and yet produced enough for two men.

The Chieftain's Son

One time, Senan and Notal went together on a journey to the place known as Cell Mor Arad Tire. When they arrived, they found a gathering of people crying aloud with sorrow for the death of their chieftain's son. When they saw the two holy men, they rushed toward them, and one, who was the mother of the dead child, fell to her knees and begged them to bring her son back to life. "Only God may do that," said Notal sadly. "My child never harmed anyone," cried the woman. "For the sake of his goodness and the goodness of the God you serve, I ask that you bring him back to me!"

Then Notal looked into the inner place where all visions are found and said, "Bring the child here." When the woman did so, Notal told her to give him into the arms of Senan. He, with fear in his eyes, cried that his teacher was wrong to ask this of him. But Notal only said, "It is given to you to do this."

So Senan took the body of the child in his arms and rocked him back and forth for a time and prayed and went inward into the secret place of his soul. Presently the boy was heard to speak, and Senan, with tears in his eyes, gave him back to his mother. Then all there marveled at the miracle, and many wished then and there to follow Senan. But Notal told them they must wait awhile yet, but to come to Cell Manach a year from then. To Senan he said, "Now are the Blessed Patrick's words fulfilled. Soon it will be time for you to leave my house and go forth on your own." But Senan was not happy at these words and sought always to cling to the place where his teacher dwelled.

After the miracle of the chieftain's son, the name of Senan became widely known in Ireland, and people flocked to see him. Once again, Notal spoke to him of departure, and of setting up his own foundation. Senan replied, in some anguish, "Dear father, it is not my wish to do this! I am not yet ready to leave you." But Notal pressed him until at last Senan agreed and prepared to go forth. Yet, still he hesitated, asking where he should go. "That is already chosen for you," replied Notal. "Nor shall I advise you, for the way that you go shall be the way the spirit guides you."

So at last, Senan set forth and followed the wandering way for a time, always finding a welcome in the hearts and homes of the places he visited. In time he came to Ferns and there remained in the company of Maedoc for a time, declaring him to be his anam cara, his soul friend in matters of the spirit.

So a year went by, and still Senan made no move to set up his own foundation. From Ferns he went to Wales and met with the great David, but the new year found him once again in Ireland, this time settling for a brief time on the island of Inis Cara, where a number of people came to join him. At last, as he lay awake one night, one of the Shining Ones appeared before him, the same that had helped him long since in the milling of corn. The bright being spoke to him and asked why he had not yet settled in a place where all who sought him could come. "I do not know where to go," cried Senan in anguish. "Whatever place my steps are led seems never to satisfy me." "Come," replied the Shining One, and he lifted up Senan and flew with him to the island named Inis Cathaig, or "Scattery" in the common tongue. There they settled upon a height that is still known as Arn na n-Aingel, "the Height of the Angel," and Senan, whose eyes were tightly closed from terror of the flight, opened them again and looked around him.

The island seemed a very fair place, but not a single homestead was there upon it.

"Why is this place deserted?" asked Senan. "For it seems to be a perfect place to build and make a life." "The reason is coming closer even now," replied the Shining One. Then Senan looked where he indicated, and saw coming toward them the most terrible monster. Its body was black and as large and long as a hillside, ending in a tail that was like that of a whale. A horse's mane it had, and a maw filled with cruel teeth, and iron claws that struck sparks from the rocks as it walked. Its eyes gleamed red and were filled with savage anger. A great heat came from it, and a stink of corruption.

When he saw the monster, Senan was fearful, but he felt the presence of the Shining One and raised his hand against the beast. It stopped and regarded him with fury and a degree of puzzlement. Then Senan spoke loudly and clearly. "I bid you depart this place," he said, "and trouble this land no more!" He hesitated. "Go to . . . Dubhloch in Slieve Collain, for this is a place where men do not go and where you shall cause no harm."

For a moment it seemed as though the monster would engulf Senan. But at last it turned away from the power it felt within him and dragged its huge bulk into the sea (it is said that the water boiled from the heat of its passing) and so to the farther shore. From there it went into the loch at Slieve Collain as Senan had commanded, and to this day it has been seen no more.

When it was gone from sight, Senan walked around the whole island, blessing every place and saining it from the dark influence of the creature. "Here then I shall make my home," he said when he had done, and the Shining One smiled and was gone.

Senan and the Druid

So Senan began to build on the island of Scattery, and people came from afar to hear him teach and to travel with him on his voyage of the spirit. But when news of this came to the ears of Mac Tail, the king of the area, he was angered beyond measure. "Who has dared to enter my lands and settle there without permission!" he cried. Then he summoned his chief steward, Coel, and sent him to remove Senan and his followers from the island.

The steward went to the island and demanded that Senan leave at once. But Senan stood his ground and refused. "For," said he, "it seems to me that your king has no more right to this land than I, seeing as it was I who rid this place of the monster." But the steward would not listen. He ordered the two men who were with him to drag Senan down to the shore and to throw him into the sea. The men dragged Senan over the rocks until he was bruised and bleeding. But Liath could not bring himself to do further harm to the holy man and refused to help his fellow do the evil deed. The two men argued there on the beach, until at last Liath picked up a stone and struck Coel down. Then he helped Senan rise from the stones.

"You should not have done this deed," said Senan.

"Even though it was to help you?" answered Liath.

Senan shook his head. "Nevertheless, I thank you," he said.

"What will you do now?" asked Laith.

"I shall wait what comes," said Senen and sat down on the stones.

"Then I shall wait with you," said Liath and sat down beside him.

When the two men failed to return, the king's steward returned alone to the king and told him that Senan would not go. Mac Tail turned at once to his Druid and demanded what could be done.

"I shall take a charm to him, and he shall either die or leave the island," said the Druid.

The king was well pleased at this, and the Druid set off at once. When he came to the island, he found Senan waiting for him.

"Leave this place," said the Druid.

"I shall not," answered Senan.

"Then I shall make a spell against you."

Senan answered with a charm of his own:

> *I shall resist your spell.*
> *Disgrace shall be upon you.*
> *You shall be wretched forever.*
> *It is you who shall perish.*

...

"My powers are greater than yours," cried the Druid, though he drew back a step.

"You will do no good," answered Senan. "Whatever you do shall be turned away."

Then the Druid called a darkness over the sun, so that the island was as black as night.

At once, Senan called forth the sun again, so that it shone brighter than before.

The Druid responded with thunder and lightning, which shook the earth. But this too Senan put away, so that the sun shone and the storm clouds lifted. Then the Druid became enraged. "I shall go from here," he said, "but you shall not see me go. When I return, it shall be with such power that you may not withstand it."

"Go then," said Senan, "but you shall have no luck where you are going."

The Druid called up a thick mist in which he wrapped himself as if it were a cloak, then he went away to an adjacent island, where he began to make mighty spells and call his forces to him. Senan knew all of this and went to the shore and touched the sea with his hand. At once the waters rose up and covered the island where the Druid had gone. He was swept away and drowned for all his magic, while Senan returned to his hut.

Senan and the King

When the king heard what had happened, he was more determined than ever to see Senan put forth from his land. He went himself in his finest chariot and with his finest armor and took a ship to the island, where Senan awaited him.

"So you are the one who has taken my island from me, and who slew my Druid."

"You forget that it was I who caused the monster to depart," said Senan. "While it remained, no man could come here."

"Nevertheless, the land is still mine," declared the king angrily.

"What man may truly say that he owns any part of the land," answered Senan. "Surely it is for all men."

"Yet, you shall go from here," answered the king.

"You have not the power to make me," Senan answered mildly.

"That we shall see!" ranted the king. "I care nothing for you! No more than for a swarthy, hornless sheep!"

With that, he set off back to the land, where his chariot awaited him. He determined to gather men and return to drive out Senan by force. But as they drove toward the king's palace, a black, hornless sheep burst out of the bushes at the roadside and startled the horses. The king was thrown from his chariot and, striking his head on a stone, died instantly.

The manner of the king's death was perceived as a sign of Senan's power, and he was henceforward left in peace, the king's relations declaring the island his in perpetuity.

The Drowned Children

After this, people came from far and wide to join Senan. He began to take pupils, and they in turn took others. One of Senan's closest followers, Donnan, had two young boys whom he was teaching to read. On a bright day in spring, they went down to the seashore to gather seaweed. While Donnan's attention was elsewhere, the two boys took a small coracle and set out on their own adventure. But the sea rose against them and they were drowned, their bodies washed up like driftwood on the shore.

Donnan's agony was great, as was the children's parents, who came to the shore and stood weeping over the bodies, seeming no more than asleep on the warm sands. Then first Donnan, and after the parents, called out to Senan to bring the children back to life, as he had done long since with the chieftain's son. Senan stood in meditation for a time, then he bade Donnan speak to the children and tell them to rise. Fearfully, Donnan did so. At once the children sat up and began to speak. Seeing their parents there, they reproached them.

"It was no good thing to bring us out of the land where we were," they said.

"Why," said their mother, "would you rather be in that land than with us?"

"It is the finest place that ever there was," answered the children happily. "Everything is filled with golden light and music, and we can play for as long as we wish without ever growing tired. Do not ask us to return to this land."

Then both the parents wept, for they knew they had indeed lost their children. But Senan said to them, "Do not be sorrowful! I promise you that you shall not feel the pain of loss." Then the children lay down again and spoke no more, and Senan and Donnan took them back to Scattery and buried them there with the consent of their parents, who in truth felt but little grief through the intercession of Senan.

The Holly Well

Soon after this, there was a year of great drought, and on the island there was little or no water. Every day, Senan's followers bemoaned the lack and begged him to perform some miracle or other for them. Senan always hung back from this, until one evening as he sat alone, one of the Shining Ones who were ever his companions came to him. "Let us go forth and discover a place where a well may be sunk," said the angel.

So Senan and his companion went to a place near the center of the island where there was a hollow in the earth. "Dig here," said the Shining One. Senan dug with a branch of holly that he found lying nearby. As he worked, the angel cleared away the earth, the pair laboring side by side in silent companionship.

Soon, fresh water began to bubble out of the earth. "This well shall not run dry while you or your fellows continue to live here," said the Shining One.

Senan planted his holly staff there in the earth, and it at once took root. Next morning, he came with his companions to draw water, and they found a fully grown tree beside the new well, which seemed as though it had been always there. Thereafter, as the angel had foretold, the well was always full of fresh water for the brethren of Senan.

The Coming of Canair

One day as Senan walked by the shore, deep in meditation, he saw a figure coming toward him across the water that divided the island from the mainland. As the figure came nearer, he saw that it was a woman. She stood upon the water as if it were dry land.

"Well, I am here," she said.

"Who are you?" asked Senan in astonishment.

"My name is Canair," said the woman.

Then Senan knew her as one justly famed for her wisdom, who lived in the south of the land, in the territory of the Benntaige.

"You are welcome," said Senan. "Nevertheless, women do not come ashore here."

"I have heard that all are welcome in the houses of the Celli Dé," answered Canair

"Nevertheless, bid you to go and seek the fellowship of women," said Senan. "There is a foundation not far from here."

"It is my understanding that women as well as men may enter the Land of Promise," said Canair. "I have come far to meet you," she added, "and to die here.

Shall I get what I desire?"

"You are stubborn indeed," said Senan. Then he laughed and bade her come ashore.

"I shall not trouble you for long," said Canair.

With Senan's permission, she made herself a hut there close to the shore, and there she lived out her last days, dying shortly after and being buried in the graveyard of Senan's foundation. In that brief time she became firm friends with Senan, and they spent many hours together. When her death day came, the wise man was sorrowful, though he knew that she would enter the Land of Promise without hindrance, and that in truth he would soon follow her.

The Death of Senan

So the time came when Senan knew that he was destined to pass from this life, and so he went on a last pilgrimage through the lands of Ireland and Britain to greet those whom he called soul friends for one last time.

For several months he journeyed, then turned for home. Within a few miles of the craft that would take him across to Scattery, he passed through the woods of Cell Eochaille. There, as he drew close to a great and ancient thorn tree, he saw a Shining One standing in the road. "It is time, Senan," said the angel gently. At once, Senan's face lit up. Turning to his companions, he said, "I must leave you my friends. See that my body remains here this night, then take me home."

Senan's companions wept at this, but as he lay down beneath the thorn tree they saw a wondrous sight. Senan's body began to glow with golden light, which swiftly spread to the tree until both were bathed in it. All night the glow burned on, until with the dawn it faded and the body of Senan lay cold and still. Sadly, his companions carried him back to Scattery and buried him there. Long after, it was said that at night a glow issued from the earth at the site of his grave, and that a thorn tree took root and grew there, shading his final resting place.

Senan's name is a vital clue to the possible origin of elements in his life story. "The Old Bright One" can refer to either the monk or the sun. An old praise poem, the "Amra Senain," roughly contemporaneous with Senan's actual dates, describes him in metaphors that include "excellent moon brilliant as the day" and "a golden lamp lit by God," and mentions him sailing "around the heavens" with his followers. He may thus indeed be the inheritor of older figures, gods even, who tended the passages of the heavenly bodies as Senan tended the souls of those who followed him.

But it is as a friend of angels that Senan is best remembered. Again and again we read of him receiving help and instruction from these unearthly companions. But more than most of those with whom he shared this gift, we see the Shining Ones helping him in a very direct way, as in the presence that helps him defeat the robbers, or the physical task of digging the well on Scattery.

In fact, despite belief to the contrary, such animosity between the saints and the Druids was rare. Generally, they seem to have recognized each other as like-minded seekers of wisdom who just happened to worship different gods (or anyway, gods with different names). Magical battles like the one described above are not often found in ancient texts describing Druid fighting Druid. For example, in the text known as *The Siege of Drom Damhgaire*, there is a description of a Druid battle between the famous Mogh Ruith, who served the king of Tara, and Ciothruadh, who served the king of Munster, which is strongly reminiscent of Senan's struggle with Mac Tail's Druid.

Ciothruadh caused springs and streams to dry up in Munster, but Mogh Ruith relieved the drought. Then Ciothruadh decided to use Druidic Fire against the enemy. He ordered the king's men to go and each cut down a quickbeam (mountain ash or rowan) and make a great fire from the resulting wood. If the smoke drifted south, then Tara would overcome him, but if it came northward, then Munster would overcome him.

Mogh Ruith perceived their purpose and ordered the men of Munster to bring out of the forest a faggot of rowan wood. Then he ordered that the king should himself bring out a special bundle of wood that had grown in the shelter of three things; sheltered from the northeast wind of March, sheltered from the sea winds, and sheltered from the winds of conflagration that were being lit against them. Mogh Ruith's apprentice, Ceannmhair, built up this wood in the shape of a triangle, with seven vents into it (Ciothruadh's fire was heaped up only roughly, with three vents). Then Mogh Ruith asked each of the Munster troop to give him a shaving from the handle of his spear, which he then mixed with butter and rolled into a great ball, saying all the while:

I mix a roaring powerful fire;
It will clear the woods; it will blight the grass;
An angry flame of powerful speed;
It will rush up to the skies above;
It will subdue the wrath of all burning wood;
It will break a battle on the clans of Conn.

Then he threw the ball into the fire, whence it exploded with great force. Saying that he was about to bring a rout upon the enemy, Mogh Ruith told all to stand ready and watch if the fires blew northward against their foe. Then "he blew his druidical breath up into the sky, and it immediately became a threatening black cloud, which came down in a shower of blood upon the plain before him and moved onward from that to Tara, the Druid all the time pronouncing his rhythmical incantations."

Mogh Ruith asked what effect the flames were having, because he was blind. They reported that the fires were chasing over each other west and north, and that not a tree in mid-Munster was left standing. When he asked again, the fires had risen up into the sky like angry warriors. "Then Mogh Ruith called for his dark-grey hornless bull's hide and his white speckled bird headpiece, and he flew up into the air to the verge of the fires and commenced to turn them northward. When Cormac's druid, Ciothruadh, saw this, he also ascended to oppose Mogh Ruith." But Mogh Ruith knocked Ciothruadh to the ground and turned the fires north, whereupon Cormac's army retreated, hotly pursued by Mogh Ruith in his chariot drawn by wild oxen.

This may seem a far cry from the life of Senan; yet, we can see a number of parallels between this Druidic battle and his own struggle with Mac Tail's Druid. As so often in this collection, we see that the storytellers who wrought the stories of the Celtic saints drew heavily upon the stories of their predecessors. In Senan's tale there is the mysterious haunted mill, which, though here the account makes it an angel who is the mysterious helper, we can easily see how an older story of the mysterious invisible miller helped an older hero grind his corn.

Throughout Celtic tradition, as elsewhere, mills were considered sacred and full of an ancient potency, and Senan is only one of many of the Celli Dé who are associated with mills and milling. The idea behind this is perhaps one of spiritual refinement. As grain is processed in the mill, so souls are refined in the "Mill of God," the experience of the world. The fact that Senan is helped by a Shining One is another way of saying that we also, each one of us, are helped—or can be if we are willing.

From birth to death, Senan is accompanied by angels. He lives ever close to the borderlands of the spirit, speaking of it even while still a babe in arms. From there it is possible to see past, present, and future as a whole—something that we can learn to do only with difficulty but that, once achieved, leaves us changed forever. We may not literally believe in angels, but to act "as if" we are aided through our lives by unseen helpers is to bring an extra dimension into our lives in terms of the shamanic teachings that are so much a part of the lives of the Celtic saints, the invisible companions, cowalkers who attend us through life and aid us at moments of greatest need. From here to the concept of "guardian angel" is a very small step indeed.

Senan moves though his life with a sturdy sense of destiny; there is a shapeliness to his life that mirrors that of all soul-full people. From the beginning he is destined to find his way to Scattery and build there. The monster that prevents anyone going there before, which "does God's work" as Patrick says, reflects the way that we are sometimes prevented from fully appreciating what is in store for us—our vocation is not a territory into which we need to rush at once; it is a guarded territory that awaits a fully committed approach.

Senan's own life reflects this. For a long time, he is fearful of committing himself to the role of teacher and wiseman for which he was born. We too can be afraid to accept the gifts and blessings that are given to us, and it may take time before we can do so. Yet, once we do we enter ever more fully into life, we can perceive the spiritual present in everything—surely one of the greatest gifts we can know.

Not for nothing is Senan described as

a glassy well whereby all who entrusted themselves to him were washed by the purity of his teachings . . . a heavenly cloud whereby the earth and the souls of those followed him were watered by the rain of his virtues . . . a golden lamp lit by God; . . . a precious stone from which the heavenly palace is built upon earth; a pure vessel by which God's wine is dealt out to the people; a great and happy hospitaller of good fortune." (Amra Senen)

This last metaphor, of the "great and happy hospitaller" who offers spiritual hospitality to all, is perhaps the most fitting for this wise and holy man, whose welcoming in of Cenair alone sets him apart from many of his fellows and who dwelt on the borders of the spirit and dispensed good will and generosity of the soul to all who found their way to him.

MEDITATION POINTS

- Do you offer hospitality of the spirit to those around you?
- If not, consider how you might do so.
- Are you ever aware of angels watching over your life?
- How might they seem to you if you were to describe them?
- Do you ever cross into the borderlands of the spirit, and if so, what does this feel like?

Amra Senain
(Dallan in His Blindness)

Bright-eyed Senan,
Swift-flowing dispenser of virtue;
Singular master; wonder-bringer;
Protector of secret wisdom;
Vessel foaming forth words forever;
Who gives bountiful rewards,
Whose treasures are brighter than gold—
May he, the grandson of Dubthach,
Many branched scion of saviours,
Save me, my sight, and my soul.
May my darkness be broken wide,
May I see again, discover words
Otherwise lost forever.

Idle prisoner of my loss,
I find my way by pronouncing
Senan's name alone. Before:
My verse, eclipsed, my voice
Silenced; after: fogs dispersed,
My words in blossom.
May he save me,
The Old Bright One,
Who watches the heavens,
Ageless and eternal,
Filling the rivers
With bounty of stars.

(Attributed to Dallan Forgail;
version by John Matthews)

•••

SIX

THE GIVER OF ALL GIFTS

MOCHUDA OF RAHEN
(August 19)

*A great household could not be better
Than my oratory in Tuain Inbir.
The stars are familiar to me there,
The sun and moon
In their usual places . . .
(Anonymous, ninth century. Translated by J. M.)*

...

Mochuda, or Catharch as he is sometimes called, was born in Castlemain, County Kerry, around 570 CE. Adopted by Bishop Catharch the Elder, whose name he may possibly have taken later on, he adopted a hermit existence at Kiltulagh before establishing a community at Rahan in Offaly at around 595. He was for a time apprenticed to the great teacher Comgall at Bangor. He wrote a verse rule that is still extant and that he seems to have received from an angel. In 635, he was expelled from Rahan by Blathnat, the local ruler. He led his community to the banks of the Blackwater and laid the foundations of a great monastic settlement at Lismore, where he is still regarded as the tutelary Bishop. That he was not always popular is suggested by the story of the two British monks who tried to murder him in the belief that they should have a new leader, but on the whole he seems to have been a mostly saintly man, who could refuse no request and gave of his remarkable gifts unstintingly. In his life story he comes across as a determined man who went out of his way to deny no one and whose attunement with the natural world produced some astonishing miracles. The story of the rivalry between his foundation and those of surrounding areas rings true historically; there was no central organization within the Celtic monastic communities throughout Ireland, and disputes and rivalries undoubtedly sprang up from time to time. As with so many of the life stories of the Celtic saints, there are distinct signs of borrowing from older sources, as in the story of the giant Constantine, whose exploits equal those of many an ancient hero.

Two prophecies concerning the coming of Mochuda are recorded. A Shining One spoke to Comgall of Bangor, telling him that a child would be born to his race that would have a great future, and with whom he would spend a year of his life. On another occasion, Brendan heard of a child who would be named Catharch. Neither knew when and where this would come to pass.

Now it happened that there was an assembly of the tribe of Fegus mac Roich in Ciarraige Luchra, and to this went Figenius, who was a direct descendent of the Fergus, together with his wife, Med. The woman was with child at that time, and that night, as the tribespeople gathered in the great hall, a globe of fire was seen by all to descend upon her and hover above her head. On all sides there was great astonishment, and the Druids proclaimed that a great one was about to be born.

Soon after, Med gave birth to a son, who was named Catharch, which is to say, "Dear One." From the start he was gifted with great gentleness and sweetness, so that everyone loved him. When he was old enough, he was taken to an aged bishop who bore the same name, and this good man took him into his house for fostering. "This child is my portion of goodness," the old man announced, and thus the boy became known as Mochuda because in Irish "my portion" is written "mo chudid." When word of this birth came to Brendan, he knew that the prophecy was come to pass, and he wrote and told Comgall of the event.

Mochuda spent much of his childhood days employed in herding swine, along with the other children of his village. One day all the herdsmen went to the royal fort, and Mochuda went with them. Somehow it came to pass that the king noticed the boy and began to take a special interest in him. The queen, when she saw this, asked her husband what it was about the herd boy that fascinated him. "Can you not see?" the king answered in awe. "There is a crown about his head and a pillar of light that reaches up to the sky above him. Mark my words, this is a Child of Wonder that is among us."

Then the king called Mochuda to him and said, "You have the right to bear arms as did your father. I will give you the best weapons and honors ever given to any man if you remain here and become part of my wear band." But Mochuda shook his head. "You are generous, my lord, but I prefer the open land and the company of birds and beasts. Nor shall I raise my hand against another in anger or war."

The king was impressed even more by the youth's words and was sorry indeed to see him go. But "if it is your wish," he said. Then Mochuda surprised everyone by taking the king's hand in his and touching him on either shoulder, knee, and foot. "Why do you do this?" demanded the king. "Any limb that I have touched this day shall never be hurt in battle nor suffer disease," said Mochuda dreamily, as though he spoke from another place. The king and all those present looked with awe upon the boy, and many now saw the light that was about him in those moments.

The Wondrous Apple Tree

After this, word of Mochuda's gifts spread, and people came to see and hear him. But Mochuda became restless and set forth on a wandering way for a time. First, he went to Comgall, who told him of the prophecy he had had years before, then he went to visit Ciaran, who told him that one of the Shining Ones had spoken with him but three nights before and had told of his future. Eagerly, Mochuda asked what had been said, and Ciaran revealed that there was a place in the heart of Ireland named Rahen that was destined to belong to Mochuda. "There you shall remain for twenty years until you are expelled. Then you shall build a foundation at Lismore and there live out your days."

When he heard this, Mochuda went aside into the wilderness to be alone and to consider these things. There, as he sat in contemplation, came a man named Magus.

"You are the one they call Mochuda?" he asked.

"I am," replied Mochuda.

"I hear you can perform miracles," said Magus.

"It is not I who do them," said Mochuda.

"Nevertheless," said Magus, "I would see some of your wonders."

He pointed to an apple tree that stood nearby. "There should be leaves on that tree."

At once the tree was thick with leaves.

"It would be even better if it had blossom upon it," said Magus.

Mochuda looked at the tree, and blossoms sprang out upon it.

"Ha!" said Magus. "What use is a tree without fruit."

Mochuda stirred slightly, and the tree became laden with apples.

"They are not very ripe," said Magus.

At once the apples turned red as gold and fell in a shower around the tree.

Magus picked up an apple and looked at it. Then he took a bite and at once spat it out. "There is no point in having a beautiful fruit if it's sour," he said scornfully.

With a sigh, Mochuda blessed the apples, and at once they possessed all the sweetness of honey.

"That is better!" cried Magus and ate several of the apples.

Then a strange look came over his face, and, stretching forth his hands, he cried out in terror that he was blind.

Mochuda took his hands and placed them upon the man's eyes, and with that he could see again. Now he fell down at Mochuda's feet and begged forgiveness for his doubts and foolishness. Mochuda raised him up and embraced him, and after that it was said that wherever Mochuda went, there Magus went also.

The Journey to Rahen

After this, Mochuda began his journey toward Rahen. Along the way he met many people who begged him for help, and he always did what he could for them. In one place he healed a madman, in another he raised a dead child to life, and in yet another he gave back speech and hearing to one who had been stricken deaf and dumb. Elsewhere he healed a leper. Wherever he went, it was said that he would refuse no one anything if it were possible—and many things were possible to Mochuda that another might not have done.

One day when they were near the ford of Owenmore in Munster, Mochuda found an apple floating in the water and picked it up. They went on their way for a time after that, until they were in the country of the king of Fermoy. Now it happened that the king had a daughter, who was paralyzed in one arm, and when he heard that Mochuda was coming that way, he went and begged him to perform a wonder and heal his daughter. When Mochuda saw the girl, he took the apple out of his robe and offered it to her. The girl stretched out her left arm to take it. "No," said Mochuda, "stretch out your other arm." Wondering, the girl obeyed, and for the first time in her life she was able to move her right arm and take the apple. The king gave thanks and offered lands to Mochuda, but he would not be turned aside, for Rahen had been set aside for him and he would go nowhere else.

When he was still several days' journey from Rahen, a Shining One came to him and told him that he must go more speedily since the king of that land was dying, and only Mochuda might heal him. "It will take me three days at least to get there," said Mochuda. "Not with my help," answered the Shining One. Then he lifted Mochuda up and flew with him and set him down closer to the king's hall. Mochuda was able to save the king's life that night, and as a reward he had permission to build at Rahen.

Constantine the Giant

First among those who came to offer help in the work of building work was a man named Constantine the Pilgrim, a giant of a man who was of royal blood but chose to wander the land helping those who needed it. His strength was great, but his appetite prodigious, and though he did the work of ten men, he seemed to eat the food of twenty. One day he was outside digging a trench, and it happened that the rest of the community went to eat but forgot him. When he realized what had happened, Constantine flung a shovelful of earth over the roof, so that some of it went in through the openings that had not yet been covered, and into the plates and cups of those within. The commotion that ensued brought Mochuda himself to deal with the problem. He found Constantine in the trench, sweat running down his brows. Mochuda smiled at his hardest worker and himself wiped some of the sweat from his brow. "Your sweat will always heal people from now on," he said. And so it was, for afterward it is said that anyone who touched Constantine when he was working and got some of his sweat upon them, if they were sick they were at once made better.

Expulsion

So the foundation grew apace, and word of Mochuda's teachings and wondrous acts went out through the land. People began to flock to Rahen, until it was hard to sustain them all. One day a man named Lasianus came to see Mochuda and secretly brought with him thirty cattle that he intended to offer to the community. But first he wanted to test Mochuda, so he pretended to be unwell, saying that he could drink only milk—this in the knowledge that there were no milking cows in Rahen. Mochuda brought forth a flagon of water, and as he walked he spoke words of blessing over it. When he handed it to Lasianus, it was filled with milk.

After this, many others came with gifts, and soon the foundation was the richest in the neighbourhood. Thus the leaders of other, smaller communities began to feel envy toward Mochuda, calling him proud and greedy and other unworthy names. Soon a party of these envious men went before the new king of the area—the old one having died—and petitioned him to expel Mochuda, giving as reason many vile calumnies and lies against him.

The new king, whose name was Blathmac, was inclined to believe the slanderers and went with his brother Dairmait, who was a king in his own right, to expel Mochuda and his followers from Rahen. When he saw them coming, Mochuda asked Constantine to go forth and meet with them. "Ask them to grant me a year before I must leave," he said.

Constantine went forth with his great club in his hands. When the two kings saw the giant coming, they looked at each other.

"I have come to ask a year's grace for Mochuda," said Constantine mildly.

"It is granted," said Blathmac, and the two kings returned home.

So the year passed, and soon the kings returned, this time with more men.

Again Mochuda asked Constantine to ask for a year, and again he went forth. The kings pretended not to see him, but Constantine went right up to them and said, "This is neither wise nor polite. Once I had as many as seven kings at my command, and more sheep and cattle than all of you. Now I have nothing but the clothes I stand up in and this club. This I do for the love of God and Mochuda. Will you talk with me?"

"We will grant you another year," said the kings, and they went their way.

So the time passed, and at the end of that time Blathmac and Dairmait returned for the third time. Once again it was Constantine who met them. This time they decided to be firm with him. "You will get no greeting from us," they said, "unless you and all who dwell here are willing to depart."

Constantine walked up to the two kings and seized them both by the neck, one in either hand. "Unless you grant Mochuda another year's grace, you shall be covered in each other's brains," he said gently.

"It is granted," gasped the kings, as best they might.

The Founding of Lismore

Sadly, soon after this, Constantine died. Great was the mourning of all, for he had been much loved. Now, without him to protect them, the community was driven forth, and Mochuda led them along the hot roads of midsummer until he reached the territory of the Deisi. The king of those people, who was named Maelochtraig, gave them permission to stay, for that very day his wife had told him of a vision in which she saw a great flock of birds settling on the land, and one, which seemed to be their leader, on the king's own shoulder. "That will be Mochuda and his people," said the king, and he went out to welcome them.

So the community settled there and began to build a great foundation at a place called Lismore, which was indeed the very place where it had been foretold that Mochuda would one day come. There he grew old, and there, one day, as he was sitting in the sun watching his followers struggling to cut a field of corn, Mochuda rose to his feet and said, "Soon, I must leave you all, but there is one final gift I may give you. You may have more reapers to help you." Then, it is said, a company of the Shining Ones came among them and cut the corn for them, while they marveled.

Soon after, Mochuda died, and many who witnessed it told how a great company of angels came to meet him and carried off his soul in a blaze of glorious light. After his death, many wonders were performed in his name, and men continued to say that no request made to Mochuda was ever refused, if it were possible.

Mochuda was a giver throughout his life. Whenever anyone asked for anything, he tried to give it—whether it was the strange challenging Magus (clearly either a Druid or a magician), who demands the apple tree be given fruit, blossom, and flavor, or the multitudinous requests for sight, hearing, speech, cures for leprosy and paralysis, and much more. Of course, all the saints were asked to perform miraculous cures, and most of them did so, but none perhaps as unstintingly as Mochuda.

The most interesting character in the story, however, is Constantine, the giant pilgrim who not only does the work of ten men (and has the appetite to match) but protects Mochuda and his followers from the incursions of their envious neighbors and the kings of the area. There is little doubt that Constantine is based on one or other of the older Celtic heroes, such as Cuchulainn perhaps, though he is a far less gentle character than Constantine. Perhaps one of the several figures in Celtic myth who derive from the Greek hero Hercules may be the real origin of this wonderful character?

One such candidate in particular leaps to mind—Ogma, to whom is attributed the creation of the mystic Ogam alphabet, a device used by the bards and Druids to pass messages between each other and to invoke the gods. In one text, this character is referred to as Ogma Cermait (Honey-Mouthed) and Trenfher (Strongman, Champion). The classical author

Lucian wrote that he was the Celtic Hercules, and gives a description of a painting that depicted an ancient figure drawing a group of men chained by their ears to his tongue. Puzzling over this, Lucian found a native Celt at his side who was willing to elucidate:

> We Celts do not agree with you Greeks in thinking that Hermes is Eloquence: we identify Hercules with it, because he is far more powerful than Hermes. And don't be surprised that he is represented as an old man, for eloquence . . . is wont to show its full vigour in old age. . . . This being so, if old Hercules here drags men after him who are tethered by the ears to his tongue, don't be surprised at that either: you know the kinship between ears and tongue. ("Heracles")

Ogmios's title Trenfher suggests an actual identification with Hercules/Heracles, whilst his Hellenized name means "the Walker," and if we recall that the original meaning of the word "pedant" is derived from scholar, or "one who walks up and down," we may see how this follows. Constantine, who walks the roads as a pilgrim and seeks to serve others, seems a perfect descendent of Ogmios and offers yet another example of the way in which the writers of the saints' lives drew upon older material.

Mochuda is a giver of all things. His generosity begins with the spirit and extends outward to include all his fellow creatures—in which he includes animals and birds, those whose company he prefers, as do so many of his fellows. Drawing strength from the inner world of the Shining Ones, as well as from the natural energy of the land and its inhabitants, he is able to offer the greatest gift of all: unconditional love. This is perhaps the hardest thing we can encompass in our own lives, to give all and ask for nothing in return. Yet, with practice, we can accomplish much, beginning with small gifts of kindness and building slowly, at our own pace, to larger acts off generosity and love. That this is hard for us to do is partly because of the way we live today. We are encouraged to think only of ourselves and nothing more. Yet, if we move beyond the often-self-imposed barriers of selfishness and self-centeredness, we will begin slowly to open ourselves to the place where we can serve others also. This is Mochuda's deepest message to us, and one from which we can learn a great deal on our own journey.

MEDITATION POINTS

- Do you consider yourself a giver?
- If not, consider what it would take to make you into one.
- Do you hold back from giving of yourself, and if so, why?
- What would you consider the greatest gift that you could give another?
- Think of three examples of times when you have received an unqualified gift of the spirit.
- What differences, if any, are there between gifts of the spirit and ordinary gifts?

The Voyage of Cormac Mac Culennan

Shall I choose, O King of the Mysteries,
After delighting in downy pillows and sweet music,
To go upon the rampart of the sea,
Turning away from my native land?

Shall I be poor in battle,
Through the grace of the undying king,
Without honor, lacking my chariot,
Without gold, silver, or horse?

Shall I launch my dark coracle
On the broad and glorious ocean?
Shall I go, O King of Heaven,
Of my own will on the brine?

Whether wide or narrow,
Whether served with hosts or not,
God, will you stand by me
If I go to the angry sea?

(Anonymous, eighth century; translated by J.M.)

...

SEVEN

FIRE OF THE SPIRIT

SAMTHANN OF CLONBRONEY
(December 19)

*May my soul be filled
With the elemental manna of God,
And may Samthann of Clúain Brónaig
Bless me with her mighty host.*

The Martyrology of Oengus
Translated by John Matthews

...

Not much is known about the life of the eighth-century St. Samthann of Cluaiun-Bronaigh (died ca. 739). A brief biography, written in Latin and dating from the fourteenth century, is the basis for what we can say about her, and is the source for this retelling. The origin of the manuscript, probably based on much-earlier recensions, seems to have been in the Longford/Westmeath region, which, since the monastery ruled over by Samthann was in county Longford, makes sense. Samthann was not the founder of this community but seems to have followed on from an earlier abbess, Fuinech, her remarkable abilities very quickly pointing her out as someone possessed of great vision and spiritual fire.

Samthann is of particular interest because she is one of a small handful of women who ruled over a monastery—the others including St. Bridget of Kildare (pp. 61–75) and St. Íte of Killeedy. Unlike these extraordinary saints, who flourished in the sixth century, Samthann dates from the eighth, when the originally independent Celtic church was beginning to be subsumed by Roman Catholicism. Her story demonstrates how, at a time when women were given very little real power, it was still possible to shine the light upon the world and to bring about some extraordinary events. Her life, as chronicled in the Vita Samthann, shows her as determined, fierce in defense of others, and gifted with a deep visionary sight that enabled her to see past the surface of reality into a place where miracles could occur. The story of the giant eels, as told below, shows her standing up for the rights of women and the defense against rape, at a time when such concerns were rarely noticed or acted upon. Determined to avoid an arranged marriage made for her, she entered a monastery by her own choice. Like Senan of Scattery (pp. 95–109), she is often referred to as being like the moon, and her followers as stars. The vision seen by the Abbot Lasran, the founder of a monastery at Devenish in Lough Erne, at her death seems to confirm this.

A striking aspect of Samthann's mysterious power is her ability to produce simulacra—doubles or images of living people or animals that appeared real but were actually copies. In the life of Samthann we see this several times—first in her giving a calf to a desperate leper, which is then apparently doubled, and later when a prisoner is at once seen in the hands of his captors and actually going free elsewhere. Such abilities were noted among several Irish saints during the sixth century.

Another of the most intriguing aspects of her life, which may be referenced in the Vita, is her apparent connection with a remarkable saint named Fergal, better known as Vergilius of Salzburg. This extraordinary man, who was an early proponent of the round-earth theory, earning him the disapproval of several popes, may be the nameless baby born out of wedlock whom Samthann adopted and raised in the monastery. Even if this is not the case, such adoptions were not unusual at the time, and Fergal/Vergilius's name is linked with Samthann as a longtime spiritual anam chara *or soul friend, who continued to advise him until her death.*

Another connection was with a founder of the Céli Dé movement, which sought to strengthen the Celtic church just before it became subsumed by Rome. It's claimed that Samthann heard of a young monk named Maelruin and that she sent a message to him asking him to become her soul friend. Blushing, the monk declared himself most happy with this, and thereafter they exchanged messages over a long period of time.

As we have seen throughout this collection, an older, pre-Christian story may well lurk just below the surface of the eighth-century text. The eighteenth-to-early-nineteenth-century writer Sylvester O'Halloran (1728–1807), chasing down the origin of the name Samhain, was led to believe that Samthann derived her name from Senae, an ancient order of women that he compared to the Druids.

> Thus Samothes appears, I think, with great probability, to have been an Irish deity, and his worship to have spread from hence, with Druidism, to Britain and the continent. Besides this, [the Roman author] Pomponius Mela tells us of a female order of religious among the Gauls, dedicated to one of their deities, who made vows of perpetual celibacy; and their votaries were called Senae . . . these Senae must have been the priestess of Sambuin, and from them I conjecture that some of our antient females

might take names, as they do now from Christian saints; thus, among our early Christians, I find, a Saint Samthann, Abbess of Clon-brone, whose life is yet extant. [spelling modernized.]

...

Another interesting detail is Samthann's association with an ancestor known as Fiatach Finn mac Dáire (ca. 36–39 CE), who according to medieval Irish legend and historical tradition was a high king of Ireland, and an ancestor of an early medieval Ulster dynasty, the Dál Fiatach, who ruled over central Ireland in the Middle Ages. This would have given her family a very high status in Ireland, even as late as the eighth century, and may well explain the significance of her refusal to accept the marriage arranged for her by King Cridan (a monarch of whom no references are found outside the life of Samthann).

All of this suggests that Samthann could well be a memory of a more ancient figure, though this cannot be proven unequivocally. In all, we must admire Samthann both for her determination, occasional shafts of humor, and very human wisdom as well as for her almost magical abilities.

Samthann's parents were Diarán, son of Ferdoman, and his wife, Columba, who were of the lineage of Fiatach Finn, lord of Erin. But as was often the way at this time, she was fostered by Cridan, the king of the Uí Coirpri. Such fostering meant that the king had the right to give female children in marriage to men of rank. One such noblemen had seen the young Samthann and desired to marry her, and King Cridan agreed. So a marriage was arranged, but Samthann was reluctant, for she had already received visions in which she dedicated herself to God.

On the night before the wedding was to be celebrated, the man to whom she was to be married saw her in the hall where she slept with the king's two daughters. As he looked, although it was deep midnight, he saw that a ray of light had entered the room through a small window and now fell across the sleeping girl's face. This pleased the man greatly, since he saw it as a sign that his wife was blessed.

Next night, when the solemnities had been celebrated, the two retired to their marriage bed. There the husband asked her to undress so that they might be united, but Samthann begged him to wait until everyone else was asleep. To this he agreed and in a while fell into a sleep himself, while Samthann prayed to God to release her from the marriage.

Then a remarkable thing occurred. A pillar of fire settled upon the hall and quickly spread to each house in the dun. To the eyes of those living there, it seemed that the whole place was on fire, and they rushed outside and began to collect water to try to douse the flames. Samthann and her husband also left the house, and, in the confusion, Samthann escaped and hid herself in a brake of ferns.

Soon after this, the flames vanished and the people of the dun were amazed that no damage had been done, and knew that the fire was of no ordinary kind.

Meanwhile, Samthann's husband discovered his loss and came before the king to demand that he produce her. The king, believing that something was taking place that had nothing to do with the everyday world, agreed and soon set forth himself in search of Samthann.

He found her among the ferns and asked her why she had fled.

"I did not ask to be married," she said. "Nor did you ask me."

The king was surprised by this, since it was not the way of that time for women to refuse marriage. But just the same, he looked at the young woman before him and saw that there was a light in her such as he had never seen, and so he said that he would dissolve the marriage and that the decision of what to do with her life would be hers.

"It is not my will, but God's," she answered. "But I thank you all the same."

Then Samthann declared that she wished to enter a monastery, and to devote her life to serving God—and so it was done. Samthann entered the house of the abbess Cognat, at Urney, which means "the place of prayer" and is placed in the county of Tyrone. There she became the abbey's steward for a time, caring for the welfare of the sisterhood and all who visited the monastery.

But it was soon evident that Samthann had within her the fire of heaven, for in her first days at the house of Cognat she performed several miracles. Once, when a leper appeared outside the walls of the convent, Samthann went out to bring him across the river that flowed past. As they were crossing, the man complained of his lack of possessions—even a cloak to keep out the cold. At once, Samthann gave him a calf from the stables and cut her own cloak in half to cover him. Next day, when the man had left with much gratitude, the same calf was found in its own pen, and Samthann's cloak was as if new.

At this time a certain cleric came to stay at the monastery. While he was there, he became enamored of one of the young postulants and persuaded her to follow him into the woods nearby, where they might enjoy the delights of love. But in order to reach the place of assignation, the man had to cross the river. When he waded into the water, a giant eel rose from the depths and attached itself to his privy parts, coiling its body around him so tightly that he could not get free and found all movement difficult and painful. Terrified, the lustful cleric somehow made his way back to the monastery and there came to Samthann and confessed his intention. After which he begged forgiveness, and only when Samthan gave it did the eel fall from his body.

Kings and Warriors

Not long after this, the king of Connacht and the king of Tethba, who had been at war for some time, made a treaty, and to serve this the king of Tethba took a youth who was to serve as hostage for the agreement. The youth's mother appealed to Samthann for help, and the fire-lit woman sent words to the king asking that he set free the youth. This the king refused and set out to cross the Shannon River to Connacht. But as the messages from Samthann were on the road back to Cognat, suddenly they saw the youth among them, while the king's guards, who thought they had the hostage fastened in his restraints, suddenly found the manacles were empty, though still fastened. At this, the king of Tethba accepted the will of God and sought for another hostage to seal the bargain.

Nor was this the last time that Samthann intervened in the affairs of kings and princes. On another occasion she heard of a man named Fallomain who had been imprisoned without reason by King Cenenétig. Deeming this to be a false and unwise act, Samthann sent a messenger to ask that the prisoner be released. But the king refused, asking, "What right does this woman have to make such a demand of me?"

Samthann's messenger then requested to see the prisoner, which the king allowed. To him the messenger said, "Believe that the promise made by Samthann will happen as she has declared it will. You will walk free this night."

When he heard this, the king ordered the guards to be doubled and further fetters to be added to those already holding the prisoner. In the middle of the night, Fallomain awoke to find that his chains had fallen off him and that the door to his cell stood ajar. He walked out and was challenged by the guards, who asked him who he was. When he told them, the guards simply laughed at this, saying that if he was truly Fallomain he would not saunter past so calmly.

Avoiding the second set of guards, the prisoner climbed over the wall and escaped. When he heard this, the king, despite his anger, praised the light that shone from Samthann and promised that Fallomain could return to his old life.

After this, many people came to the monastery to consult with Samthann to discuss spiritual matters, or simply to ask for her blessing. One such was a warrior named Flan, son of Conla. Whenever he intended to go into battle, he always requested Samthann to bless him. But one day he went into battle without doing so and was killed. At the moment when this happened, Samthann called her sisters to pray: "Flan has died unshriven in battle, and his spirit is even now wandering in a dark place. Let us all pray for him that he may find the path to heaven." Then Samthann entered into a trance, and when she awoke she told her companions that Flan's spirit had been guided by their voices, raised in prayer, until he entered the path that would guide him to the company of God.

Departure from Cognat

Soon after these events took place, the founder of the monastery of Cluaiun-Bronaigh, the blessed Abbess Fuinech, had a dream in which sparks of light surrounded the house and turned into flames that seemed as if they would consume the whole place. And in the sparks, Fuinech saw the face of Samthann, so that when she awoke and found the buildings untouched, she declared that by this sign the divine fire burned within Samthann and that henceforward she should lead the community.

So it was that Samthann traveled to Cluaiun-Bronaigh and became the abbess of the house following Fuinech's death. From this time, many new novices began to arrive at the monastery. Samthann decided to build a great hall to house them. And she sent the prioress Nathea and some craftsmen into a nearby woods to cut down timber. For several days they wandered in search of pine trees, which they favored to build the hall. But they found none. But Nathea had a dream in which Samthann came to her and said, "In the morning, go to where you will find bog willow growing and cut these down. You will find that when they are fallen, they will have become the pine you seek."

So it was done, and soon there was a great heap of wood. At this the owner of the land came there, and when he saw the pine wood, he demanded payment. Nathea asked that he wait one day, and that night she again dreamed of Samthann, who told her that all would be well. And on that same night, the man who owned the woodland saw Samthann in a dream. "Do you know only greed?" asked the wise abbess. Then she struck him on his side with her staff and told him that unless he gave the wood to her sisters he would suffer.

When he awoke, the man at once gave Nathea permission to take the wood, and when word of this came to the ears of the local community, they provided teams of yoked oxen to convey the timber back to the monastery.

Nor was this the only time that Samthann demonstrated a particular association with the trees of the forest. One day, two people came to her who had produced a child out of wedlock. Fearing the shame this would bring upon them, they requested that Samthann adopt the child and raise it within the monastery. This she agreed to do, and the child is believed by many to be the famous Fergal of Salzburg, who was one of the first to believe that the earth was round, and was one of the founders of the Céli Dé or Brotherhood of God.

On their way home, the couple were pursued by a band of robbers. Fleeing into a woods, they sought shelter. And there, a great tree opened itself to them so that they could hide in its interior, and closed itself around them in protection. At the same time, a thick mist formed around that part of the forest, until the robbers had departed, after which the mist vanished and the tree opened up again, allowing the travelers to continue unscathed.

At another time, when Samthann was traveling back to the monastery with a group of her sisters, a huge oak had thrust a mighty branch across the road, preventing their passage. Uttering a prayer, Samthann pushed against it with her staff, and at once the branch coiled back upon itself, allowing the abbesses' party to pass.

When these stories were told to Niall, son of Fergal, who was king of Ireland at this time, he wished to have Samthann's staff decorated with gold and silver and sent a craftsman to do this. At first Samthann was reluctant to allow this, but her visions told her to let it take place. When the craftsman saw the staff, he declared that it was not worthy of his skill, so twisted and ancient was it, but that night the staff became straight and strong, and the man was duly penitent and completed his task.

The Last Days of Samthann

For many years thereafter, Samthann ruled over the monastery, and her fame spread through Ireland. Toward the end of her life, the monks of Iona sent to her a boatload of wool. On the way, the ocean became much disturbed and the sailors believed they would be drowned. One cried out that "the wool for the old woman" should be thrown overboard to prevent them from sinking, but another crewman declared that the wool must be kept for the saintly lady. With these words the sea became calm and the wind dropped. "Couldn't the old one send us wind," said one of the mariners, and at once the sails filled so that they reached harbor without further trouble.

When they arrived at Cluaiun-Bronaigh, Samthann came to meet them. She smiled at the man who had suggested throwing the wool over the side and said, "What was that you said about my wool when death threatened you?"

The man hung his head in shame.

"Whenever you are in fear, you may call upon me," said Samthann.

Throughout the remainder of her life, Samthann maintained the monastery of Cluaiun-Bronaigh with courage, honesty, and determination. In all that time she shared the divine fire that filled her, and when the day came for her to depart the realm of Earth, the Holy Abbot Lasrán of Devenish, who had spoken often with the abbess, saw two moons in the sky, one of which dipped toward him. Then he smiled and remembered how Samthann had told him, long before, that when she passed into the starry realm, she would bend toward him. "This is Samthann departing this life," the abbot said, and so it was.

But none forgot Samthann's spiritual fire, which made the world a fairer place for that time, and within a few years of her passing she was declared a saint.

Samthann's advice was widely sought by people from all walks of life and all levels of society and was always practical. One day a certain teacher named Daircellach came to visit her. He told her that he was going to stop studying and praying because he intended to go on pilgrimage to the Holy Land. Samthann looked at him in wonder and said, "It is not necessary to travel afar to find God, since He is in everything. You may reach heaven from anywhere on the earth." Another time a monk asked her what was the best way to pray—prostrate, upright, or seated. Her reply was that whatever position one adopts, it is the intention of the prayer that should concern us. She was, above all, someone who devoted herself, body and soul, to her beliefs. Whether or not we are ourselves believers in the same way or of the same things, we can learn from her unswerving loyalty to the things that matter most—the spiritual underpinning of all life.

MEDITATION POINTS

- What light inspires you? It does not have to be divine, but what do you look to when making important decisions?

- Samthann's relationship to the natural world was considerable. What do you feel when you step outside your door into a garden or walk in nature?

- Where does your spiritual life begin and end? How important is belief to you and how much does it influence the choices you make every day?

- To what sources do you go in search of healing?

- Who is your soul friend?

To Samthann

*The following poem is adapted from
that written in ca. 734 CE in celebration
of Samthann and attributed to the
eighth-century king Aodh Allán, son of Fergal.
The poem praises Samthann's courage
and determination while living
the monastic life.*

...

Remember Samthann for her bright light,
Who served God with her powerful dream,
In Meath of the wide and fertile plain
Samthann endured the greatest of hardships.

Hard were the things she undertook
Fasting in honour of heaven's light.
Living on bread and water,
Her garments harsh and rough.

Struggling against cruel adversaries
Her heart remained pure and true.
Her death, when it came, was simple
As she passed from this strident earth.

(John Matthews after Charles Johnston in *Ireland,
Historic and Picturesque* [Philadelphia, 1901])

...

EIGHT

THE FRIEND OF THE SPIRIT

DAVID OF WALES
(March 1)

The road to old St. David's
Is the white road of the blest . . .
When all the wandering roads of Wales
Went winding to the West.

A. G. Prys-Jones, "A Song of the Pilgrim Road"

...

Given his popularity and importance as the patron saint of Wales, surprisingly little is known about David. He was born about 520, reputedly the offspring of a casual mating by King Sandde of Ceredigion and Non, who herself went on to become one of the best-loved saints of Wales. He is first mentioned in an eighth-century Irish document known as the Catalogue of the Saints and again in the slightly later Irish Martyrologies. These state that his chief monastic foundation was at Menevia, believed to have been located where the present-day St. David's Cathedral stands in the city of Cardiff. In fact, he may have begun his career in a monastery at Hellan in Dyfed (Pembrokeshire), which he received as a gift from his father. He is also said to have founded a settlement at Glastonbury, one of the many great saints claimed by that center of myth and tradition, and possibly as a result of this he is also said to have been the great nephew of King Arthur.

David is mentioned in several other lives as a mentor or soul friend to Maedoc of Ferns, Senan of Scattery, Findbarr of Cork, and Brendan of Clonfert. The picture of monastic life contained in the eleventh-century account of David written by Rhygfarch is believed to be a particularly accurate one, with its emphasis on personal toil in the fields and farms, abstinence from all liquors save water, and the daily round of prayer and contemplation.

In the life, David comes across as a strong-willed man dedicated to the work of learning and teaching. The strictness of his regimen—he often used to stand up to his neck in icy water for hours at a time—has led to a belief that he himself was cold and unsympathetic. However, nothing could be further from the truth when one reads the story of his life, with its many magical and soul-driven acts, such as the curing of his teacher's fading sight or the wonderful episode in which he enables the visiting Findbarr to cross the ocean on the back of a horse, which could have stepped from the pages of a far more ancient tale.

Known familiarly to the Welsh nation as Dewi, a pilgrimage to St. David's—performed twice—was considered equal to a journey to Rome. This practice is still followed today.

Son of the Sea

One night as he lay abed in his palace at Ceredigion in Wales, King Sandde awoke to the sound of a voice speaking in his ear—though he could see no one in the room. "Tomorrow," said the voice, "you shall go hunting. Near the river you will kill a stag, and in that place you shall find three gifts: the stag itself, a fish, and a hive of bees. Send these to the foundation of Maucanus, where they shall be kept for a son that shall issue from you."

The king was fearful at this, but on the morrow he set forth as the voice had instructed him, and sure enough he chased and killed a great stag, and at the spot where it fell next to the bank of a river, he found a fish lying on the bank, while overhead a hive of bees hung buzzing in a tree. Marveling, Sandde commanded his followers to take these three things to the nearby monastery of Maucanus, while he himself returned to the palace alone. As he followed the road close to the sea, he happened to pass a young woman who was so beautiful that the king was instantly inflamed with desire for her. There and then, against her will, the king raped her, then went on his way, leaving her behind. The girl, whose name was Non, had been a virgin until this time. Knowing that she would be outcast from her village, she went her way alone, wandering the roads of Wales until she found a small, sheltered cave on the shore of the sea. Here she made her home and waited the coming of the child that was soon kicking within her.

One day she made her way to a local church where the famous teacher Gildas was speaking to a great gathering of people. As soon as Non entered the church, he was unable to speak a word and by signs indicated that he wanted to be left alone. Everyone went out of the church except for Non, who was curious to see what would happen, and hid behind a pillar. For a while she watched Gildas struggle to speak. Finally, he was able to say, "Someone is hiding here. Come out at once!" Shyly, Non emerged and at once the man's tongue was loosed. He asked the girl who she was, and had her story from her. "I believe the child that grows within you will be a great teacher," he said. "For in the presence of such a one I am silenced!"

King Sandde meanwhile had learned from his Druids that the child whose coming had been foretold by the mysterious voice would be born to the girl he had taken so casually on the road. Now he set out to seek her and soon learned of the strange wild girl living in the cave by the sea. It was at this very time that Non felt the onset of her birth pangs. Driven by a need she could not express, the girl left the cave where she had been living and sought the place where her child had been engendered. As she went, the sea rose and the heavens opened and rain deluged the place. Lightning flashed, thunder rolled, and hail lashed the earth with whips of ice. Weeping, Non hastened on as best she might, until she reached the spot where King Sandde had found her. There, to her wonder, was a meadow where the sun shone, the rain fell not, and the earth seemed as soft to her as a bed. Here she gave birth, grasping a stone that was said to carry the marks of her fingers ever after. And here King Sandde found her, cradling her newborn son to her breast. The king knelt beside her and begged her forgiveness. "This child is destined for greatness," he said. "If you let me, I will care both for it and for you."

Non agreed and returned with the king to Ceredigion. Ever after, it is said, her child, who was given the name of David, loved the sea and went there whenever he could, so that in time to come he was often called "the Son of the Sea."

A Gift of Sight and a Prophecy Fulfilled

Once her child was old enough to be put out to fosterage, Non returned to the place where she had given birth and there set up a small cell in which she lived out her days, becoming known throughout Wales as a wise and holy woman famed for her gifts as a healer—especially to sicknesses suffered by women in childbirth. David was fostered with a wise teacher named Paulinus, in a place called Menevia. There he learned to read and write and began to study the mysteries. It is said that it was at this time that he befriended a dove, which afterward went everywhere with him, sitting on his shoulder, and was even believed by some to teach him the secrets of the world. It was also at this time that he performed his first wonder.

When David had been at Menevia for several years, his teacher, Paulinus, began to suffer with inflammation of the eyes. When this became so bad that he could scarcely see, he called all his pupils to him and asked them to bless his eyes, hoping that they might be healed by the touch of caring hands. When David's turn came, he hesitated, and when pressed he admitted that in all his time at the school he had never once looked his master in the face. Moved by this show of humility, Paulinus said, "Without looking, raise your hand to my eyes. I know they will be healed." David did so, and at once his teacher could see again as well as he ever had.

Not long after this, one of the elders from the foundation of Maucanus came and spoke of a dream he had had. In this dream, one of the Shining Ones had come to him and showed him three things that had been sent to them years ago by King Sandde. These were meat from a stag, together with a huge salmon, both miraculously preserved, and a hive of bees that had continued to give great quantities of honey ever since the king's men had brought it there. These, the angel told him, were intended for a youth who even then was a pupil at Paulinus's school.

When he heard this story, the teacher knew at once that the youth must be David, and sent for him. Tears sprang to his eyes when he learned the story of his father's vision, and it was agreed that he travel back with the visitor to Maucanus. Once there, after much thought, David prepared a meal with the flesh of the stag and the salmon, cooked in honey from the beehive. This he served up for all who were guests of the foundation, and it was said that never was there such a feast in all that part of the land. Afterward, David returned to Menevia, bringing the hive with him. Many saw a change in him and spoke of a new sense of purpose that he had. Thereafter he loved to keep bees, and when he finally ended his wandering days, there were always hives on hand to feed the community.

The Death of Dunawd

Thereafter the fame of David's miraculous gifts began to spread, until his teacher declared that it was time for his pupil to set forth and begin the work of founding schools of his own. Reluctant at first, David set out on a pilgrimage through the land of Britain, visiting many of the foundations already set up by the Celli Dé. Yet, though he constantly sought to find a place where he might settle, always one of the Shining Ones would speak to him, telling him that another place awaited him "beyond the next hill or valley." Over a year after leaving Menevia, he was close to home again, and there at last the Shining One told him of a place nearby where he was destined to be. A small, sheltered valley, it lay in the shadow of a huge crag named Clegyr Fawr, on which stood a fortress belonging to an Irish freebooter named Boia. The spot to which David was led, which was called Glyn Rhoslyn, had long since been marked out for settlement by St. Patrick, but the great teacher had been turned away by his own angelic guide, who told him, "This place is destined for another, who shall be led here in time to come and will do great wonders in this spot."

So David and his small band of followers began to work to tame the wild land and make it ready for those who would come. Thus it was that they came to the attention of Boia, who, truth to tell, cared little for who might settle on his land, so long as they left him in peace. Boia's wife, however, was incensed by the presence of the Celli Dé and insisted that her husband go forth and drive them out.

Boia arrived at the small circle of huts where David and his followers were living, and demanded that they leave. But David stood his ground, and such were his gentle ways that Boia found himself giving permission for the work to continue, providing that the settlement spread no farther than the valley.

Boia's wife was furious when she heard this, and she set about her own plans for driving out David and his slowly growing band. Her first plan was to send all her maids to bathe in the stream near the settlement, hoping that the presence of laughing, naked girls would cause them such embarrassment that they would leave willingly. Indeed, the monks were at first put out by this, but David told them to be patient: "They will soon tire of this sport, and once the weather turns cold, they will stop coming."

And so it was, but Boia's wife did not relent in her animosity toward the Celli Dé. Her next plan was both desperate and dark. She sent word to her stepdaughter, who was named Dunawd, to come and visit her, and when the girl came, she took her to a lonely spot farther up the valley in search, she said, of hazelnuts. When they had been there for a time, the woman lay down, feigning tiredness, and invited Dunawd to lay her head in her lap. Then, as the girl slept, Boia's wife took out a knife and cut her throat, so that her blood flowed into the stream. Then she cut off the girl's hair and made an offering of it to her gods.

Somehow she believed that this terrible act would cause the community to vanish away entirely. But when it failed to have any effect, and fearful that the murder of Dunawd would be discovered, the woman crept out of the fortress at night and fled way, never to be seen again. That same night, a rival pirate named Leschi crept up to attack the fort. Finding the gate open, left that way by the fleeing woman, the pirate entered and slew everyone therein, including Boia, who died in his sleep and without even having time to draw his sword.

When David heard of these events, great sorrow overcame him. He went to the place where Dunawd had been killed and there blessed the earth. A small spring of clear water began to bubble out of the ground, which thereafter was known for its curative properties.

Honey and Wild Horses

David's small community became famed for its strict regime. David insisted that his followers should be self-sufficient, breaking the land by dragging the plough themselves, milling their own flour, planting and harvesting what they needed to feed themselves and those who came to visit. Their daily routine of prayer and meditation became a model for many who came after them, and the simplicity of their way of life became the fulfillment of all who sought to follow the path of the Celli Dé.

David himself remained especially fond of bees and kept several hives that were the descendants of the one discovered by his father. One day, Modomnoc of Leinster came on a visit from Ireland to Menevia. He remained there for some weeks and spent many hours helping David tend the bees. When it came time for him to depart, a swarm of bees followed him and attached themselves to the prow of his ship.

Not wanting to deprive the community of their precious cargo of honey, Modomnoc walked back to Menevia, with the bees following. When he saw what had happened, David laughed: "Evidently my bees like it better where you are going. Let them go and take my blessing with them, that they grow and increase in your land." With that he blessed the bees, and Modomnoc returned with them to his ship. It is said that thereafter the bees of Leinster were more plentiful and gave better honey than in any other part of Ireland. Modomnoc himself said that the community of Menevia was itself like a hive, whose honey was pure wisdom and the wonder of David's inspired teaching.

Many other visitors found their way to the sheltered valley—among them Findbarr of Cork. He remained with David for a month or more, discussing everything from the names and virtues of the stars to the nature of the Shining Ones. Eventually the time came for Findbarr to return home, but he was prevented from departing by contrary winds that kept his ship penned in the harbor for day on day. Findbarr began to fret about the delay, visualizing all kinds of disputes and quarrels that might have arisen in his absence. Then one morning he came to David and begged a favor of him. "That horse you used to ride everywhere on. Do you still have it?"

"Why, yes," answered David, puzzled.

"May I borrow it for a while, and will you give the animal, and myself, your blessing?"

"I will do both, and most willingly," replied David.

Findbarr mounted the horse and rode straight down to the shore of the sea. Here, to the astonishment of everyone, he kept on going into the water and was last seen riding across the tops of the huge waves as though the sea were a level plain.

With wind and rain lashing him upon every side, Findbarr rode on across the ocean toward Ireland. On the way he met with Brendan, who was engaged on his own voyage of wonder and was at that moment riding the back of the great sea creature Jasconius (see chapter 1). There Findbarr paused for a while, and he told Brendan about David. "Truly these are wondrous times," said Brendan, who promised to visit Menevia himself when his voyage was done. Then Findbarr went on his way and soon arrived back in Ireland, having ridden all the way on the back of David's horse. When he told his own companions of his journey, they were filled with wonder and thereafter cared for the horse until the day of its death. Afterward it became a saying that as the sea had horses, so had David of Wales his own wondrous steed.

The Passing of David

For many more years, David continued to teach in Menevia, which expanded to become a settlement of some size. In addition, he set up other foundations of learning and wisdom and traveled widely throughout the lands of Britain. Once, when he was copying a page of the Gospels in the scriptorium, the bell rang to call the community to prayer. David left the page half done but, when he returned later, found that it had been completed in letters that blazed with gold. For many years after, the book was kept hidden at David's bidding, but after his death it became famed throughout the land, and people came from great distances to see it.

But in time David grew old, and there came a day when, sitting in his cell, he received a visit from one of the Shining Ones, who told him that the day was approaching when he should pass from this life. David greeted the news with delight and told his followers, who were greatly cast down.

"Do not be sad," David told them. "This is a day I have longed for all my life."

Thereafter as the day drew near, David spent his time preparing himself for his death. And, none knew how, word of his imminent passing spread throughout not only Britain but Ireland also, and people began to come from all over these lands to pay homage to the holy man. Like bees they gathered to the hive of Menevia, which was made abuzz with the voices of those who wished to see David one final time.

On the fifth day of March, he gave one last address to the gathered people, bidding them, "Do these little things we have spoken of." Shortly after, he became seized with pains and was carried to his cell, where he died that night. Afterward, many bore witness to the fact that the building was filled with light and with a singing that could only be that of the Shining Ones themselves, and thereafter many wonders were wrought in the name of David of Wales.

In nearly every instance, births of saints are announced or predicted, either by angelic informants or through other signs and wonders. None perhaps as dramatically as David, whose coming is foretold by the gifts of a stag, a fish, and a hive of bees. All

three were considered sacred among the Celtic peoples—the stag for its strength and otherworldly appearance (Arawn, the lord of the Underworld, sometimes rode on a stag); the salmon for its association with the story of Fionn mac Cumhail, who ate of such a sacred fish and imbibed wisdom with it; bees because they were considered to be oracular creatures and guardians of the land's bounty. Singly these images might mean little; collectively they say very clearly that a child of wonder is coming.

This, together with the dramatic nature of his conception (though he is not alone among the saints to be born illegitimate; Kentigern is another), single out David as an important figure, whose credentials would have been recognized both by pagans and Christians—a useful attribute in a time when the two spiritualities often clashed with each other.

The story of the sacrifice of the girl Dunawd is a further example of the way in which those who forged the lives of the saints strove to echo earlier tales, shaping them to their own needs while remaining true to the original. At one time the slaying of the girl might well have taken place in a ritual setting. The use of it here as a story device is further extended by the aftermath: the evil woman vanishes, her husband is slain, and a spring of healing water rises where the girl died. There is even some evidence that Dunawd may have been revered as a saintly person herself and that she was the center of a minor cult in the area where these events were believed to have taken place.

There is also the matter of David's wonderous horse, which is able to cross the ocean as though it were on dry land. Among the Celtic deities, Manannan mac Lir, the god of the sea, possessed such a horse, called Aenbarr; no rider was ever killed while on its back. Many of those listening to the story of the saint would have recalled this miraculous beast and its owner.

David himself is portrayed as a late starter, full of modesty and gentleness. The episode in which he restores the failing sight of his teacher is typical of the shyness that he strove to hide in later life but perhaps never completely overcame. His dying words, in which he bids his followers to remember the "little things" that he had taught them, rings true. David's teaching, like the rule that he established in all his monastic foundations, was simple in the extreme and did indeed serve as a kind of exemplar to other communities.

In his desire to serve God as directly as possible, David reduced his approach to the utmost simplicity: daily prayer, meditation, and a strict honoring of the canonical hours. Simple food, simple words, simple truths. Yet, how profound these could be! As with all the Celtic saints, David lived close to the natural world, emphasizing the need to till the soil with his own hands, to be self-sufficient as far as was possible. In our own time we have only recently begun to appreciate the need to live in this way, and though it may be true that we can probably never all be self-sufficient in this way, the honoring of the earth is more important today than ever before. The effect of this is to bring us into the curve of David's own truth and practice.

As well as being a child of the sea, David was known as "the Waterman," in part at least because of his refusal to drink anything other than water. Aside from this, there is a deeper meaning to this name. David can also be seen as one who ferries the souls of the living across the water of life and into the service of the Spirit, who brings those who follow his way into a quieter harbor where the spirit can grow and flourish unimpeded by the speed and complexity of life. Water cleanses all things and quenches our deepest thirst. At certain times in our lives, if we are fortunate, and quiet enough, we are able to drink from the sacred well, whose waters can spiritually refresh us.

MEDITATION NOTES

- Ask yourself how you could live a more simple life within the world.
- How would the world seem to you if everyone were able to live more simply?
- What things can you personally imagine doing without to make your life more in keeping with the simplicity of David's teaching?
- What stands in the way of your path to simplicity?
- How can you drink from the waters of life?

A Medieval Sequence of
St. David

David, splendid star,
Shines over Britain;
His sacred converse
Adorns Menevia.

Proclaimed by angels;
by Stag, honey,
fish and flowing water,
Signs that showed
His immanent nascence.

Champion of Britain,
Teacher to the Cymry,
Seeking sanctuary
In the wild vale's
Sheltered places.

Sea's Son named;
Healer, teacher,
Spiritual friend;
Acclaimed by all,
His name remembered
Ever after.

(Fifteenth-century Hereford Missal,
version by John Matthews)

...

NINE

THE LADY OF THE BEES

GOBNAIT OF BALLYVOURNEY
(February 11)
···

We know very little of Gobnait's life, since no vita has survived. However, despite this, she left more physical signs of her existence than many of those recorded here, and there is a good deal in the folklore record of Ireland that enables us to reconstruct the activities of this most unusual of women.

Gobnait is believed to have lived in the sixth century, which is in line with the explosion of saintly activity throughout Ireland at this time. The number of wells, mounds, and suggested gravesites associated with her, which have been uncovered in recent years, demonstrates that she undertook a wandering life of the kind called *perigrinatio*, whose practitioners literally followed where the spirit led. It is unlikely that Gobnait took to the seas as did Brendan and others, but there is, curiously, a tradition that says her father may have been a pirate.

The primary site for St. Gobnait is of course Ballyvourney, where the site of her foundation was excavated in 1950, when the village raised money to erect a statue to the saint on the site believed to be where her cell had once stood. The archeology uncovered there included the remains of some 137 forges, dating from the sixth century and earlier, which go a long way toward explaining Gobnait's association with metalworkers. Her name, which echoes that of the Celtic metalworking god, Goibniu, suggests that at some time she may have been acknowledged as a goddess in the same way as St. Bridget, but there is no actual proof of this beyond the associations in the land itself with her name. Interestingly, her recorded escape from her pirate father involved her commandeering a small craft known as a *naomhóg*, or little saint.

Certainly, Gobnait has far more significant sites connected with her name than almost any other saint in Ireland. Amanda Clarke, who spent years tracking down the holy wells in county Cork (see further reading), lists numerous sites associated with Gobnait, including St. Gobnait's Well at Dunquin, another at Kilgobnet, and the mysteriously named Tobar a'Rúin, or Well of the Secret, at Garfinny, where local legends describe Gobnait arriving on a wild night on a white horse and blessing the village against the effects of severe thunder and lightning. Several of these are listed as pagan sites that have been taken over by later Christian worshipers. In all, sites relating to Gobnait have been discovered at—among others—Waterford, Kerry, Munster, and the Dingle Peninsula—again suggesting the widespread honor of the saint.

The association of Gobnait with bees seems to go back a long way. Among the Celts, St. Brigid was also associated with bees and may have shared this with Gobnait. While it seems unlikely that the bees sent to her from a sister foundation in Wales were "the first worker bees in Ireland," this testimony indicates the antiquity of the tradition. St. Madonnac of Cambria, recorded in the folklore of county Cork, from whom Gobnait received the gift of bees, does not seem to have existed, though this fading of her memory may simply be due to the passage of time.

The long-held link between humankind and bees can be seen in several prehistoric cave paintings from Spain, while in Egypt there are depictions of beekeepers on the walls of several tombs, showing that bees were kept in hives as long ago as 2400 BCE. Indeed the temple dedicated to the Egyptian goddess Neith was known as the "House of the Bee," and the goddess herself was often depicted wearing a type of transparent veil that could also be seen as wings.

For this reason, Neith was sometimes titled hymenoptera, which means "veil-winged." Other Egyptian deities included the Apis Bull, which was believed to have given birth to the first bees, and there are references in early Greek myth that suggest a belief that bees were born from the body of a slain bull. This idea was later reflected in the biblical myth of the lion from whose body Samson took sustenance and strength in the form of honey from the hive that had been built into its carcass.

All of this points to a long-held belief that bees are mystical creatures, and they are present in the foundation creation myths of several countries, while the long-held belief that certain kinds of honey—especially the famed manuka honey—has powerful healing properties was widely believed throughout the ancient world. To this day, in Ireland and other parts of Europe, it is customary to "tell the bees" when someone dies or is about to die. Not long ago, the present author took part in a burial ceremony that took place close to where a colony of bees were swarming. The day before the ceremony was to take place, the bees moved to another place, returning only after the internment of ashes had taken place. Gobnait's wonderful use of bee-magic to defend her friends is a magical event that links her with spiritual traditions of many countries.

Gobnait was the Lady of Bees, for they followed her and obeyed her wishes. She was born in county Clare, it is said, of a family that traced its descent from a high king of Ireland, Conaire Mor, in a distant time. Tradition says that Gobnait's father was a pirate who raided along the coastal lands from Kerry to Munster. The girl herself was forced to accompany her father on some of these voyages, but she had already begun to experience visions and sought to escape from him. Her chance came when her father's vessel anchored at a small island off the coast, which tradition says was Inish Oirr, now known as one of the Arran Isles.

The crew went inland, presumably in search of booty, and entered an isolated stretch of woodland. There Gobnait saw her chance and ran off, hiding in the woods until her angry parent gave up and left her behind. There it was that one of the Shining Ones, who are called angels, appeared to her and told her that this was not the place where her true life would begin, but that she should journey in search of it, looking for a site where she would find nine white deer grazing.

Gobnait heeded the words of the angel and undertook a *turas*, a sacred journey that led her to many different parts of Ireland. Many were to follow this thereafter, and the roads taken by the saint may still be traced to this day. One of the first sites she came to is still called St. Gobnait's Wood. There she saw three white deer grazing, but this did not stop her, and she went on until she saw six white deer by a sacred well. But still she continued on until she arrived at the kingdom of Muskerry and there saw nine deer grazing on a hillside overlooking the river Sullane and looking toward the Derrynasaggart Hills. Beside this was already established a settlement of monks and a small village of farmers and fishermen.

Here Gobnait found that St. Abban, who is said to have been her brother, had set up a foundation, and here she decided to stay and make her own place, where women could come in search of peace and a settling of the spirit. Soon after this, the holy man became sick and died, but before he did so, he gave the care of the monastery into Gobnait's hands.

When the people heard that Abban was dead, a most powerful keening was heard upon all sides. Gobnait happened to be nursing a man who was close to death, and the healers told her that any noise could hasten the poor man's passing. Therefore Gobnait prayed deeply, and from her spread a circle of silence that could not be broken, which some say still holds good to this day at that place.

A Foundation of Light

Now, as Gobnait prepared to raise her own foundation, she begged the local chieftain for a small patch of land. He, having heard of her remarkable abilities, agreed and offered the large tract of land. But she would accept only enough to build a church and a cell for herself. There she was to live out the rest of her days, journeying and watching over St. Abban's foundation and her own settlement, which soon began to be called Bail Bhúinne, the House of the Beloved, by those who came there. In this time it is known as Ballyvourney.

Many miracles she performed there, and soon the story of her goodness and devotions spread. Once a certain wild thief known as *An Gadaidhe Dubh*, "the Black Robber," tried to steal a horse from her. He rode as fast as he could, meaning to put as much distance between himself and Gobnait's settlement—but in the morning he found that he had ridden in circles around the church. Realizing he could not win against the power of Gobnait, he returned the horse and begged for her forgiveness. The saint gave him her blessing, but it is said that she stole the likeness of the thief and carved it on a stone, which may still be seen near the place where her cell once stood.

On another occasion, the smallpox came to the community next to Gobnait's foundation. When she heard the pains of the people, she took a strong stick and took it into a field and planted it there. Then she prayed aloud, and all the sickness went into the wood and remained there. But nothing more would ever grow in that field.

The Battle of the Bees

The local chieftain, knowing how strong and holy Gobnait was, saw to it that she was well protected and cared for in those lawless times. She herself was able to help him when he heard of Danish invaders attacking his lands along the coast. He gathered together a large band of men and set out to attack the invaders. Before he left, he asked Gobnait to keep watch over his people and to pray for his men in battle.

This she promised to do. But while the chieftain was away, a band of robbers saw this is an opportunity to raid the cattle runs. Gobnait was in the midst of setting up hives for a gift of bees (some say the first worker bees in Ireland) given to her by St. Madonnac of Cambria, when news of this was brought to her. She had in her hands a *beachaire*, a box in which the bees were carried, and she took this with her and confronted the robbers and their leader.

Gobnait begged the man that he and his fellows should leave the place and not touch either the cattle or the families left undefended by their men. For answer, the captain of the warriors laughed and raised his whip to strike Gobnait. But before he could do so, one of the bees left the *beachaire* and, flying unseen, stung the man's horse.

At once the beast whinnied and reared up, almost unseating its rider. At this, a cloud of bees emerged and flew at the attackers. It is said that some of them turned into bells, which rang out across the hills in alarm, while others took upon them the form of warriors and drove that robber band away.

Then the bees turned and flew on to where the chieftain and his men were fighting with the raiders. To them, it seemed as if a whole army of men in brown armor and helmets were coming against them, and at that they turned and fled. Then the bees turned about again and flew back to the hives that Gobnait had set up. And thereafter the honey produced by Gobnait's bees was considered especially good for healing and was much sought after.

When it came time for Gobnait to die, it is told how when the monks and sisters dug into a certain mound where the saint had asked to be buried, they found the remains of an ancient site of ironworking. Then it was that many remembered the ancient god of metalworkers, who was known as Goibniu, so that from that time onward the saint became known as the patroness of those who worked with metals, and many were the prayers offered up to her, both then and now.

Gobnait is someone who shares a deep and abiding relationship with the natural world, as do so many of the saints whose stories are explored here. In particular it is the association with bees, whose patron saint she is, that has preserved her most profound connection with these magical creatures. If you have ever studied the life of the bee or simply watched them busy collecting pollen from flowers in your garden, you are witnessing something that is hugely important to us and extremely mystical. We hear a great deal of the endangerment to the bee communities brought about by the use of chemical pesticides, and you can read in many sources about the damage to our environment that their loss would mean to us. Gobnait's magical use of bee-magic is a reminder of just how closely we are related to these extraordinary creatures, and invites us to acknowledge them in our lives. They remind us of the importance of community, of sharing work and the manna that comes from this in our daily lives. It is not the intention here to suggest you get too close and personal with either an individual bee or a colony, but observing from a safe distance and using your inner senses to communicate with them can bring about remarkable experiences. A shamanic connection, in which a bee becomes your totem, can be profound. It is always important to acknowledge the coming of such an unearthly being into our lives, though it's never acceptable to summon one without permission.

MEDITATION POINTS

- What do you feel when you watch bees at work or even just look at a picture of one?

- Consider the healing properties of honey as it might appear in your life.

- Think of any sequence of places that have featured in your life. What led you there and what, if any, are the connections between one and another?

- Undertake a peregrination around your home environment and ask what calls out to you.

- What is your personal approach to community—either of spirit or everyday relationship with those around you?

The following poem, attributed to St. Columba, suggests the active energy of worker bees.

Adiutor Laborantium
(Helper of Laborers)

Assistant of workers,
Benefactor of the good,
Custodian on the ramparts,
Defender of the faithful,
Exalter of the humble,
Frustrater of the proud,
Governor of the faithful.
Hostile to the impenitent,
Judge of all judges,
Light and father of lights,
Magnificent shining light,
Never denying to the hopeful,
Opening help to the needful.
Poor am I, a little man,
Quaking and wretched,
Rowing through the storm,
Sacredly drawing to heaven,
Towards the supernal haven.
Vital, most beautiful gate, is
Xristus; angels sing,
Yielding praise eternally to the
Zenith, proof against foes.
Towards the joy of paradise I come.

(Translated by Caitlín Matthews)

...

TEN

A VISION OF TREES

CIARAN OF CLONMACNOISE
(September 9)

Down the five roads of Erin:
By rath and bog they passed:
Ciaran of Clear was the first,
But who shall be the last?
—Patricia Lynch, "Ciaran"

...

Ciaran of Clonmacnoise came from a line of bards and poets, which may account for his love of learning and his close relationship with the natural world—especially trees, for which he seems to have had a more than usual love. He was born in the ancient kingdom of Mide (Meath), around 512 CE, the son of a chariot maker, and seems to have demonstrated remarkable qualities from birth. While still a youth he went to study at the school of another remarkable teacher, Findian of Clonard. This man, who is remembered as a poet as well as a saint, taught twelve of the most important Celtic monastic leaders, known as "the Twelve Apostles of Ireland," of whom Ciaran was one.

Ciaran himself had a wide circle of soul friends, including Colmcille, Enda of the Aran Islands, and Kevin of Glendalough. His friendship with the warrior Diarmait, son of Culain, who is a real historical figure, is also recorded. A poem included in the life of the saint predicts the future of Diarmait:

I will bear witness truly
Though your company be only one,
You shall be a great and dignified king
Of Ireland by this hour tomorrow . . .

Without rout or slaughter
You shall take Usnach;
Diarmait, the distinguished,
Gave a hundred churches to Ciaran.

...

With the new king's blessing, Ciaran founded a great community at Clonmacnoise (Cluain Mocca Nois) toward the end of 544 CE but died less than a year later, aged thirty-three, probably of the yellow plague, which also carried off Findian. The ruins of the monastery may still be seen, on the banks of the river Shannon, to this day.

Ciaran was born at Rath Cremthainn in the province of Connaught after his parents, Beoit and Darerca, fled from the heavy tribute laid upon them by the king of Ui Neill. Beoit was a carpenter and a chariot maker, and the king of Connaught was glad to make him welcome and set him to work. But when the king's Druid, Lugbrann, saw Beoit and Darerca coming toward the rath in a chariot, he laughed aloud.

"Why do you laugh?" asked the king.

"I laugh," said Lugbrann, "because of what I see coming in that chariot."

"I see only the carpenter and his wife," said the king.

"There is another," answered Lugbrann. "The woman bears a child in her womb that shall be as great a man as any now living in Ireland. He shall be a child of the tress, and he shall give a gift to your son." But more than that he would not say.

In time, Darerca gave birth, and her son was named Ciaran. He grew to be a cheerful, kindly youth, who was forever running off into the woods. Indeed, he loved nature so much that it was often said of him that he knew the nature of every plant and herb and tree in all of Ireland.

One day when Cairn was twelve years old, a horse belonging to Oengus, the king's son, died. The youth was heartbroken, for he had loved the steed better than anything else in the world, and he knelt by its side and wept long and hard. When he saw this, Ciaran's own heart filled with sorrow, and he went up to the king's son and bade him ease his sorrow. "I will pray to the great god who made the world that he give you back your horse."

Oengus stared in wonder as Ciaran took some water and blessed it and then scattered some over the body of the horse. At once the beast began to breathe again, rose, and stood again upon its legs. Oengus was so happy that he could not speak, and thereafter he and Ciaran became close friends, despite their difference in station. Thus was the Druid Lugbran's prophecy fulfilled, and many years after, when Ciaran founded his first community of monks, Oengus gave him lands, which became known as Tir na Gabra, "the Land of the Steed."

On another occasion, soon after this, Ciaran's mother scolded him for forgetting to bring honey from the hives in the village. At once, Ciaran took a jar and went outside to the well that stood near his house. He filled the jar with water and blessed it. Then he took it inside to his mother, and she found that it was filled with the purest honey.

At another time, his father sent Ciaran to a neighboring king named Furban with a cauldron that he had ordered. But on the way, Ciaran met with a group of poor folk who had nothing in which to cook their meager fare, and he gave the vessel to them. When he heard this, King Furban ordered that Ciaran be put to work grinding corn with a quern until he had paid off the debt. But when Ciaran stood by the quern, it turned of its own accord, so that everyone was astonished and afraid. Next day, a smith came from the province of Munster with a gift of three cauldrons for the king. Ciaran was set free at once and returned home.

After this, word began to spread of Ciaran's miraculous powers. Many said that he must be destined to follow the way of the *peregrini*, the wandering wise folk who lived close to God in the wilds. And so it was decided that he should go to the school of Findian at Clonard to learn wisdom and find his way.

Ciaran set out on a bright May morning just after his thirteenth birthday. He took with him a cow, whose milk would pay for his tuition. And indeed, after he blessed it, so much milk did it give that neither Ciaran nor his fellow students ever wanted for sustenance while he was at Clonard.

Miracles at Clonard

For the next few years, Ciaran remained at the school, learning everything the wise Findian could teach. But always there were wonders, marvelous and miraculous events that followed Ciaran wherever he was.

Whenever he could, Ciaran would spend his time outside. He liked to read in the open air, sitting in the shade of a great oak tree that grew near the school. One day as he sat with a book open on his knees, a mighty stag came toward him, laid itself down by his side, and offered its spreading antlers as a book rest! After that, it came every day and used to follow Ciaran about like a dog. Often, he used to lodge his books in its antlers and have it carry them for him. On one occasion, something startled the stag, which ran off with Ciaran's precious books in its antlers. That night it rained heavily, and Ciaran was worried that the rare and valuable treasures would be ruined. But when the stag returned, not a single page was damaged.

Another time, Ciaran was befriended by a fox, which used to take messages written on a slate between the youth and his master Findian. Wherever he was, animals and birds came to him, sharing in the gentle wisdom and kindness that were so much a part of his life. Even the trees, in whose shade he so often sat, seemed to bend down over him, offering deeper shade in the heat of the summer days, murmuring their songs to him as he sat lost in contemplation of some wondrous piece of knowledge.

One year, as the season turned toward winter, the school and the area around it suffered a famine. There was a mill attached to the school, and the pupils took it in turn to grind the grain to make bread. It was said that whenever it was Ciaran's turn, the Shining Ones would come and turn the wheel for him, but on this occasion, as Ciaran carried a heavy sack of oats to the mill, he exclaimed aloud: "How I wish this were beautiful wheat, so that I could make fine bread for my fellows."

When he reached the mill and opened the sack, it was filled with oats, which Ciaran poured forth into the quern. But as he turned the mighty wheel and milled the grain, it turned into the finest wheat. Filled with excitement, Ciaran carried home his sack of wondrous flour, and when he reached the school he went at once to the kitchen and baked some bread. Everyone who ate of it said it was the finest they had ever tasted, and when it was given out to some poor folk who came that way, it not only cured their hunger but made any who were infirm well again.

When Findian heard of this he spoke the following poem of praise:

Ciaran, O great heart,
Grace will always be yours.
May you have an abundance
Of all good things.

Ciaran, blessed friend,
May all wisdom enrich you
May your life ever be
Filled with wisdom and truth.

...

And soon after this, Findian, who was himself one of the wisest and holiest of men in the whole of Ireland, had a vision. He saw two moons in the sky, one golden and the other of silver. Findian declared that this referred to two great men who would be honored throughout Ireland and beyond and bring words of wisdom to many. "The golden moon is for one who shall be called Colmcille, and he shall make a foundation on Iona that shall live for a thousand years. The silver moon is for our own Ciaran, and he shall build a community at Clonmacnoise that shall be famed throughout the whole world."

When he heard this, Ciaran was troubled, for he longed for nothing more than to live at Clonard and listen to the words of his teacher, and to the songs of the trees. But in his heart he knew that the time was approaching when he must depart. Therefore, he went to take his leave of Findian and promised him that whatever place he went and whatever foundation he made would ever be linked to his old master's school. And when he heard this, Findian wept with both joy and sorrow and made a verse for Ciaran's leaving:

A marvelous hero goes from us westward,
Ciaran, son of the wright;
without greed, without pride, without anger,
Without lust, without satire.

•••

The Vision of the Great Tree

So Ciaran set forth and for a time lived a wandering life. Everywhere he went, miracles and wonders occurred, and he was remembered with love and honor wherever he went. One time he stayed for a while on the island of Arran, and there he helped dry the corn for the kilns that belonged to one Lonnan the left-handed. This man was ever somewhat envious of Ciaran and liked to argue with him whenever he could.

One day as they were drying the corn, they saw where a ship was foundering on the rocks near the shore. "Well," said Lonnan, "that ship will drown for sure—just as surely as this kiln will be fired by the strong winds that have brought death to the mariners." "Not so," answered Ciaran. "The ship shall burn, but the kiln will be drowned."

"What nonsense you speak," cried Lonnan. But Ciaran's words were proven true, for even as Lonnan spoke, a great wave lifted the ship and flung it down on the shore next to the kiln. Flames from the fire spread outward, borne on the wind, and within moments the ship was ablaze. But as for the kiln, and all the corn it contained, that was blown by the wind out into the sea and thus drowned, just as Ciaran had foretold.

After this, Ciaran traveled to another part of Arran to stay with the wise and holy Enda. And there as they spoke of many things, including Ciaran's reluctance to settle and found a place where all could come and study with him, there came to both men at the same moment a great vision, which seemed to Ciaran as though it had been approaching him throughout his life.

In this vision they saw a great tree, mightier than any ever seen in Ireland. It grew on the bank of a stream, with its roots deep in the soil and its branches seeming to more than half the land. It was laden heavily with fruit of the richest and sweetest kind, and birds and beasts and men came from all over the world to eat of them. When he saw this, Enda cried out for joy and said to Ciaran, "This tree signifies you and all the goodness and nourishment that you shall offer to the world. See, even animals and birds come to share the fruit of your tree! Observe well where it grows, Ciaran, for on this spot you shall build a foundation that shall endure for a thousand years."

Ciaran heard the echo of Findian's prophecy in these words and shivered. In his heart he knew the truth of what Enda said. Moreover, he knew the place where the great tree grew, at the place called Cluain, which lay almost in the center of Ireland. And so he departed from Enda with gentle words and set off to where he was to found his own place of wisdom and wonder.

Clonmacnoise

Ciaran traveled through Ireland, and along the way he gathered about him seven companions, men who desired to learn from him and to help him in the work he was destined to do. For a time they lived on Inish Angin, and then at a place called Ard Tiprat, or the Height of the Well. But at length they came to Clonmacnoise, and there Ciaran stayed.

Before he could begin building the foundation, he was required to ask permission of the local chieftain, Diarmit, son of Cerball, a famous warrior. In this man Ciaran found an openness of spirit and a willingness to listen, rare among fighting men. When Ciaran put forth his proposal to build a new foundation of learning and wisdom on his lands, Diarmit gave his permission at once. Then Ciaran looked at him and said, "Will you come with me and help me set up the first post in the enclosure?"

"Why do you ask me that?" said Diarmit.

"Because it is good that men of learning and kings should work together."

"Why do you call me a king?" asked Diarmit in surprise.

"Because by this hour tomorrow you will be king of all Ireland," answered Ciaran.

So Diarmit came with him, and together they planted the first post of the enclosure. And that night, the high king, Tuathal Marlgarb, was killed, and on the day following Diarmit was declared king in his place. Thus Ciaran's prophecy was proven, and he earned a powerful friend in the course of it.

And so, building went forward and within a year the foundation at Clonmacnoise was built. People began to come there from all over Ireland to sit at Ciaran's feet and listen to his wise words. And in token of the holiness of that place, and the vision he had received while on Arran, Ciaran planted a tree that grew to a great height and offered shade to generations of those who dwelled in the foundation.

Ciaran declared that a fire should always be kept burning, in token of the holy light that lived within the community. And thus it remained for several years, until it came into the mind of an evil man named Crichid to put out the flame. And this he did, and then he ran away into the wilderness, where he believed none would find him. There he met his death, being caught and killed by wolves.

Meanwhile, at Clonmacnoise, the loss of the eternal flame had been discovered. The brethren ran to Ciaran and told him what had occurred. He, rising to his feet, closed his eyes and cupped his hands as though to receive a gift. There, fire blossomed in his hands, and amid cries of wonder he carried it to the place where the flame was kept, and lit it once again. Not so much as a scorch mark was on his hands, but the light that shone in his eyes was itself like a flame.

Not long after this, word came that Findian had died in a plague then sweeping the country, and when he heard this, Ciaran said, "I shall follow him soon." No one wished to believe this, for Ciaran was still a young man and strong. But less than a month after that, he fell sick and weakened rapidly. But this time he asked to be carried out into the open and laid upon the earth beneath the trees. Looking up at the sky through the dancing leaves, he said, "The way between the earth and the heavens is hard."

"Surely not for you, Ciaran," said his fellows.

"When I am dead," he said, "preserve the spirit of my teachings and not my relics. Let my bones rather be like those of a deer that lie all open to the sun and the rain. Let me lie beneath the tree I planted so that even in death I may share its joy and beauty."

Soon after this, Ciaran breathed his last, and his body was taken to lie in the little church that he had helped build. And a day after that, Kevin of Glendaloch came there, having heard in the songs of the birds he so much loved that Ciaran was dead. He went into the church alone and told all others to keep away. Then he sat by Cairan's body and prayed for a while. And it is said that Ciaran's soul returned to his body for a brief time, so that he might speak with his great fellow.

The foundation of Clonmacnoise became one of the most famous in all Ireland, and ever the great tree watched over it, as the shining ones watched over all who came there in Ciaran's name.

Despite the attention that the ecological movement has drawn to the plight of nature, we still take it very much for granted. This was far from the case in the world occupied by the Celtic saints. They, like their forebears the Druids and shaman-poets, were as close to nature as it is possible to be. They displayed a sympathy toward all living things, animals and trees alike, which was far deeper than a simple love of nature. For them the links were established at a soul level—hence the wonderful episodes that are to be found in virtually every history of the saints that has survived. Stories like Kevin of Glendalough's relationship to the blackbird, or Ciaran's stag, which allowed him to use its antlers as a bookrest, or the vision of the great tree that impels him toward Clonmacnoise.

Ciaran's story illustrates the way that being in nature can teach as much or more than any formal learning, and that when the two things go hand in hand, the result is truly remarkable. Such a relationship with the natural world was an inheritance from earlier times and is well attested in the fragmentary wisdom of the pre-Christian world, where a whole lore relating to sacred trees is to be found.

In Ireland, for example, there were five specifically named sacred trees: the Tree of Ross, the Tree of Mugna, the Tree of Dathi, the Tree of Usnach, and the Tree of Tortu. The great compendium of land lore, the Dindshenchas, says of them:

> Eo Mugna, great was the fair tree,
>   high its top above the rest:
>   thirty cubits—it was no trifle—
>   that was the measure of its girth.

> Three hundred cubits was the height of the blameless tree,
>   its shadow sheltered a thousand:
>   in secrecy it remained in the north and east
>   till the time of Conn of the Hundred Fights.

> A hundred score of warriors—no empty tale—
>   along with ten hundred and forty
>   would that tree shelter—it was a fierce struggle—
>   till it was overthrown by the poets.

> The Oak of Mugna, it was a hallowed treasure;
>   nine hundred bushels was its bountiful yield:
>   it fell in Dairbre southward,
>   across Mag Ailbe of the cruel combats.

> The Bole of Ross, a comely yew
>   with abundance of broad timber,
>   the tree without hollow or flaw,
>   the stately bole, how did it fall?

> ...

These are enigmatic references, probably referring to cosmic world trees of the kind worshiped among the Norse as scions of Yggdrasil, the World-Ash. Another text, *The Settling of the Manor of Tara*, tells a wonderful story in which the chieftains of Ireland, having come together to discuss the seemingly overlarge dimensions of the Manor of Tara compared to their own lands, desire to learn of the original reasons for the partitioning of the land. To this end, they summon first of all two wise poets, who in turn summon five older and wiser than they. However, none of these were able to answer, and all agreed to summon the wise teacher Fintan, who gives a poetic version of the history of Ireland,

He then goes on to tell the story of an earlier assembly of all the kings and lords of Ireland, together with all their principal storytellers, brought together on the day of Christ's crucifixion by a wonderful being called Trefuilngid Treochair, the Strong Upholder.

We beheld a great hero, fair and mighty, approaching us from the west at sunset. We wondered greatly at the magnitude of his form. As high as a wood was the top of his shoulders, the sky and the sun visible between his legs, by reason of his size and his comeliness. A shining crystal veil about him like unto raiment of precious linen. Sandals upon his feet, and it is not known of what material they were. Golden-yellow hair upon him falling in curls to the middle of his thighs. Stone tablets in his left hand, a branch with three fruits in his right hand, and these are the three fruits that were on it, nuts and apples and acorns in Maytime, and unripe was each fruit. . . . "I have come indeed," he said, "from the setting of the sun, and I am going unto the rising, and my name is Trefuilngid Treochair." "Why has that name been given to thee?" said they. "Easy to say," said he. "Because it is I who cause the rising of the sun and its setting." "And what has brought thee to the setting, if it is at the rising thou dost be?" "Easy to say," said he. "A man who has been tortured—who has been crucified by the Jews today—because of that the sun stepped past them after that deed and has not shone upon them, and that is what has brought me here to find out what ailed the sun.

In the end, Trefuilngid leaves Fintan some of the fruit from the branch he carried, and it is from these that the five sacred trees grow.

Stories such as these emphasize the importance of tree lore and the way in which it is intimately related to the mystery of life itself. Trees are among the most ancient things on this earth, and as such they represent ages of wisdom and knowledge. The Irish word for "sacred grove" is translated as fid-nemith or fid-neimid, which in turn derived from an older Celtic word, nemetos, meaning simply "holy" or "sacred." This later became extended to mean a distinguished person such as a poet, a king, or a wise dignitary. What image could be more appropriate for Ciaran's ministry than *that of a great overarching tree? The links between these ancient living things and the wisdom they have seen remain deeply rooted in our own time and can teach us, if we look closely at them, the eternal relationship that exists between ourselves and the natural world.*

MEDITATION POINTS

- Consider your own relationship to the natural world.
- Go outside and really look around you.
- If you live in a city, find a park and walk there.
- Notice things about the trees and plants. Meditate on what you can learn from them.
- Remember that they are part of the cosmos as well as you.
- Ask what you can do for the natural world.
- Try to discover what it needs to restore the damage we have done to it.

A Scribe in the Woods

A hedge of trees surrounds me,
A blackbird's song enchants me;
Above my lined page
Birds make a song for me.

The Grey-mantled cuckoo
Sings in the bushes;
May God protect me—
I write well in the greenwood.

(Ninth-century Irish; translated by J.M.)

...

ELEVEN

SON OF THE STARS

MAEDOC OF FERNS
(January 31)

Ath Ferna:
The place where Maedoc will dwell
Though filled now with litters of wolves,
Will offer songs to heaven yet.
—Betha Maedoc Ferna

...

Maedoc, who was also known as Mogue or Aedh, was born in Connacht at the end
of the fifth century CE and died around 626. He began his education in Leinster but
soon transferred to the school founded by St. David in Pembrokeshire. After a number
of years there, he returned to Ireland and founded communities at Drumlane in
county Caven, Rossinver in county Leitrim, and Ferns in county Wexford, which
has continued to be the place most closely associated with him to this day. His staff,
bell, and reliquary all survive and are to be found in the National Museum of Ireland
in Dublin, and at Armagh Cathedral. He is often remembered for protracted feats
of austerity, such as living on bread and water for seven years, but the single most
interesting aspect of his life is his visionary capacity, which is best displayed in the
episode where he climbs a golden ladder to speak to the departing spirit of Colmcille.
In addition, his soul friendships with a number of other saints, including David of
Wales, Molaise of Devenish, Colmcille himself, Ita of Killeedy, and Brighid of Kildare,
show him to have been an important figure in the network of holy men and women
who maintained the spark of the new faith within the Celtic countries.

As with so many of the Celtic saints included in this collection, Maedoc had a
powerful link with the animal kingdom, being especially fond of wolves, while his

protection of the hunted stag is yet another instance of the compassion toward other living things that set the Celtic saints apart from the rest of the people of the time, who hunted both for food and sport.

The miraculous nature of Maedoc's birth, together with the title he received, "Son of the Star," show him to have inherited, as did both Ciaran and Kentigern, something of an older tradition. The wonderful prophetic poem about Maedoc, attributed to the spirit of the great hero Fionn Mac Cumhail, makes this clear enough, while the name suggests that he should be seen as a type of solar "Child of Wonder," and as a shaman-saint, able to move between levels of being and awareness just as the tribal shamans of many lands have always done and continue to do. Indeed, we can see a striking parallel between Maedoc's ascent of the ladder and the Siberian shamans who used to shin up the tent pole of a skin tent to look around them at the hidden realms, before returning with messages for the tribe. Like them, and in common with many of his fellows, Maedoc maintained throughout his life a deep sense of connectedness with the rest of the universe through accessing the invisible realm of the spirits.

There was once a king of Connacht named Setna, and his wife was Eithne. For years they longed for a child, but without success. Then one night, both dreamed the same dream: that a star fell out of the heavens into Eithne's mouth. Each told the other of this, and together they went to the chief Druid to ask its meaning. The Druid looked into the Place Within and told them what he saw. "A child shall be born to you that shall be as marvelous a being as any that ever lived in Ireland." That same night, a child was conceived in Eithne's womb, and in the fullness of time she gave birth to a son. On the night of his birth, a ray of brilliant light rested upon the house where the woman lay in childbed. It is told that on that same night, one of the Shining Ones known as angels came to Eithne and told her that her son should be a great worker of wonders. And it is also said that this being of light alone baptized the newborn infant, giving it the name Aedh.

As was the custom in those times, the child was put out to be fostered. The woman who cared for him, who was of the Ua Dunthaig, cared for him as if he were her own, and lavished love upon him. Her name for him was "My Little Aedh," which in the Irish tongue is written mo Aed oc. This name ever after clung to the child, and in adulthood he was known as Maedoc, so that his given name was all but forgotten.

Fionn's Prophecy

Meanwhile, the Druid whom Setna and Eithne had consulted regarding the sign of the star had a dream of the child in which no lesser being than the great Fionn Mac Cumhail, the greatest and wisest of warriors in all of Ireland, who had been dead for an age, came to him and put his thumb under his tooth of wisdom, by which means he used to discover all the knowledge of the world, and he said, "How glad I am that the place where my bones lie will be the center of learning and knowledge in Ireland. Many wise words shall be spoken in this place, and one who was but lately born shall speak of the mysteries of life there." And being a justly famous poet, Fionn made a song concerning all that he had prophesied, which the Druid set down when he awoke:

Ath Ferna:
The place where Maedoc will dwell;
Though filled now with litters of wolves
Will offer songs to heaven yet.
Ath Ferna of the green strand!
Excellent he who builds there;
Soul friends will come there,
It will be a place dear to all.

Maedoc and his company shall come,
Like a glitter of sun after rain;
The Son of the Star will come,
Victorious over all adversity.

It will be a sacred place,
Where many great deeds shall happen;
Muedoc and his company shall come,
To welcome the mighty king of all.

He will be a strong and bounteous prince,
A flame of fierce consuming wisdom;
Maedoc and his company shall come,
Like a wave upon the land.

...

Thus the Druid wrote, and thus many years after he showed the writing to Maedoc himself, who had indeed come to Aed Ferna, which was known then as Ferns, just as Fionn prophesied. And when he heard this, Maedoc smiled to know that the bones of the great hero lay beneath his foundation, and hoped that he felt joy in the words and songs that were sung there.

The Song of the Stag

But all of this happened when Maedoc was in his middle years. Before then, he had a journey to undertake that took him far from his home and through many adventures laden with the wonder and wisdom of the inner life.

While he was still living in the home of his foster family, he often used to spend time with the shepherds. One day, eight young wolves approached and fawned around Maedoc as though they were dogs. All were thin and wasted, and when he saw them the boy's heart went out to them. "Take eight sheep from the flock," he said, "but see that you take no more than that." The wolves did as Maedoc had told them, and when they saw this, the shepherds ran to tell his foster mother. She came forth in great anger, and Maedoc fell upon his knees and asked that he be forgiven. When the woman came and counted the sheep, there were the exact same number as before, and of the eight that had been carried off by the wolves, there was no sign.

Soon after this, Maedoc was sitting in a quiet spot in the woods, reading, when a stag came bursting out of the trees and fell down at his feet. Maedoc heard the sound of hounds in the woods coming closer, and he placed his cloak over the horns of the stag. When the hunters arrived, they saw only Maedoc and went on their way in search of their prey. When they had gone, the stag arose and belled forth its wondrous song for Maedoc.

Another time a youth named Daimin, son of Cairbre, was drowned in Loch Erne, but his body could not be found. His mother traveled throughout the land, visiting all the Celli Dé and asking them if they could tell her how to recover her son's remains. Finally Molaise of Devenish said to her, "The one called Maedoc shall come here soon, and he will help you."

So Daimin's mother waited there, and one day soon after the young Maedoc came that way. The woman fell at his feet and begged him to help her. Maedoc was still untried in his powers at that time, but her plea moved him so deeply that he begged the waters of the lake to give up the body it had claimed. And thus there came about a great wonder, for the waters of the loch parted and the body of Daimin rose up, and when he reached the shore he awoke as from a long sleep and was as whole as ever he had been.

At once the restored youth turned to Maedoc and greeted him as though they had been old friends, for even then the wondrous man used to walk in the realm of the spirits, and many who lived there knew him well.

The Transformation of Aed

After this, word of Maedoc's miraculous abilities spread far and wide, and people began to seek him out to drink of his wisdom. But Maedoc became fearful of this attention and sought to escape to another place. It is said that he traveled to Rome itself and that in the Holy City the bells rang of their own volition when he entered there. Whether this is true or not I cannot say, but it is certain that Maedoc wandered the world for a time, and that in due course he returned to Ireland and settled for a time in Rossinver in the county of Leitrim. There it was that a certain king named Aed the Black came to him.

Now this Aed was hideous beyond measure, having suffered disfigurement in childhood. To Maedoc he said, "I have heard of the miracles you have wrought, and I would ask you to do for me the greatest service possible."

"What do you ask of me?" said Maedoc.

"Give me a new face," answered Aed simply.

When he heard this, Maedoc was troubled, for he believed that such an act as this could alter the shape of fate. But there was about Aed's wish a childlike faith, and he knew also that Aed was a powerful leader who might benefit the work he desired to do in Ireland. Therefore, Maedoc called upon the help of the Shining Ones who watched over all that he did, and bade Aed lie down on the earth. Then he covered the king's head with the cowl of his own robe and sat by him through the night. When dawn came, Aed arose, and he had upon him the face and form of a most beautiful man. Then he knelt before Maedoc and begged to be baptized, which the holy man did very willingly. Thereafter, Aed took the name Aedan Finn (Aedan the Fair) to signify the new life that had come upon him, and he made over much of his wealth to Maedoc to begin building his first foundation of learning and wisdom at a place called Drumlane. Thereafter the two men became friends, and ever after the king gave all his support to the work of the Celli Dé.

Maedoc in Wales

After a time, Maedoc desired to leave Ireland and visit those of his brethren who lived in Britain. At first, Aedan was reluctant to see his friend depart, and did everything to prevent it, asking him to teach in various places and informing him of the needs for his miraculous work. But in the end, Maedoc left quietly and found his way to the coast and so took ship for Britain. Once there, he went into Wales and sought the school founded by David of Menevia. He was warmly welcomed and spent many weeks in contemplation with the stern and holy man.

The prior of David's church at that time was an envious man, and when he saw how much time Maedoc spent with his master, he set out to damage their relationship by showing Maedoc to be lazy and shiftless. One day the brethren went out to the coast to collect firewood. But by chance Maedoc remained behind, reading in the garden of the monastery. There the prior found him and berated him for letting others do the work for him. When Maedoc showed his distress at this, the prior was glad. He bade Maedoc to make his own way to the shore and gave him a lad with an ox cart in which to carry back the firewood, secretly yoking two wild and unbroken oxen to the cart. When Maedoc came there, the wild creatures became tame at once, and so they set forth. Soon they came to the edge of a bog that stood between them and the sea. The lad began to complain about the distance they would have to go to pass around the bog. When he heard this, Maedoc stretched forth his hand and a firm road opened before them. In wonder, the lad drove the cart across the center of the bog, and thus they arrived at the shore.

Meanwhile, David came in search of his friend and found that in his haste to catch up with the rest of the brethren, Maedoc had left his precious book open on the ground. At that moment it began to rain, and David noticed that around the place where the book lay, the ground remained miraculously dry. When he saw this, he left the book where it was, and set out to follow Maedoc to the sea. When he arrived, he asked Maedoc sternly why he had left his book out in the weather, and the Irishman was so overwhelmed with grief that he fell down on the sand and would not get up again. After a time, David and the rest of the brethren set out for home. On the way they learned from the lad about the new road through the bogland, and at that, David turned to speak to Maedoc, only to realize that he was not there. No one had seen him since the incident on the beach, so then all the brethren turned about and went back to where they had last seen Maedoc. There they found him, still lying upon the sand as if in a trance, while all around him great waves rose up and struck the shore, none coming near him at all. David spoke to him gently and related that his book was unharmed, then they all set off together for the monastery.

This was not the end of the envious prior's evil deeds. So bitterly disposed was he toward Maedoc that he devised a means to have him killed, and he bribed a man to do the deed. One day, Maedoc set off alone to the woods, and the man followed him. There he attempted to strike Maedoc down with an axe, but his hands stuck to the handle, and he could nowise free himself until he fell at Maedoc's feet and confessed everything.

When Maedoc returned to the monastery alone, the prior became fearful for his own life, and soon after he fled from the place. After he had gone, the truth came out and David was mindful to set the justices upon him. Maedoc shook his head. "Do not trouble yourself, master; the man will die a terrible death alone in the wilderness, and none shall know where his body lies." And it is said that this came about just as Maedoc had foretold.

Thus he remained in Britain for a time and did many wondrous deeds there, including healing the son of a king of that land, who was both blind and deaf. But in time, Maedoc longed to return to Ireland again, and so he took leave of David and set out for home.

Maedoc of the Wolves

When he returned home, Maedoc wandered for a time throughout Ireland, meeting and talking with others of the Celli Dé, especially Colmcille, with whom he became soul friends. But in time he came to a place called Disert nDaibre— that is, the Hermitage of the Oakwood—and there he elected to remain for a time and build a foundation of learned men and women. One day, not long after the building had commenced, there came a pack of wolves to Maedoc's door, and they each showed by sign and gesture that they were starving. Maedoc, mindful of that other time when he had given the gift of life to some wolves, granted them a single calf that belonged to the brethren. When they heard this, they were dismayed. "The cows will not give milk without the calf," said one. Whereupon Maedoc called this man to come close and placed a blessing on his head. "Now," said Maedoc, "go and milk the cows." And when the man went into the byre, all the cows gathered about him and licked his head as if he were himself the calf, and they gave milk readily.

Not long after this, Maedoc was on the road to visit a foundation at Shanbo in Leinster when there came to him a female wolf that was so thin it could scarcely walk. Maedoc asked a boy who was accompanying him if he had any food to spare. They boy replied that he had a fish and some bread, but that they were for his master. Nevertheless, Maedoc took them from him and gave them to the wolf, which ran off at once. The boy was now distressed at the trouble that would come to him, but Maedoc told him to bring some leaves from the forest, and when the boy did so, he blessed them and they became a loaf of bread and a fish, which he gave with thanks to the boy.

A Time of Vision

Not long after this, Maedoc was in a part of the land where the king of Ui Cennselaig was raiding. On a particular night this king fell sick, and in his fever he dreamed an evil dream that he was taken to the mouth of a cavern, where fire and darkness awaited him. And there came forth a terrible monster that seemed as though it would eat him. Then there appeared a man who stood before the monster and commanded it to retreat so that the king was saved. When he awoke, he was so afraid of what this might mean, and, at the suggestion of his advisors, sent word to Maedoc, begging him to come and explain the meaning of the dream. Maedoc came willingly, and as soon as the king saw him, he cried out in wonder. For in Maedoc he recognized the same man who had saved him from the monster. At this same moment, the king's sickness vanished, and in gratitude he promised to give Maedoc land on which to build.

The place chosen was Aed Ferna, or as it is more simply known, Ferns, and here Maedoc began to create the mighty foundation that he had always wished to have. One day the builders came to Maedoc and complained that there was not enough water to keep them all from thirst. So Maedoc told them to cut down a certain tree, and that beneath it they would find a spring of pure water. This they did, and the water proved to be the purest anyone had ever tasted, and it may still be seen today.

After this, building went ahead without interruption, and thus was the prophecy of Fionn mac Cumhail that one called Maedoc would build there proved to be true, and in time Ferns became one of the greatest of such places in the whole of Ireland. As for Maedoc himself, this was a time of fulfillment and vision. Fulfillment because he was at last realizing his greatest wish, and vision in that he had many such inner seeings in the years that followed.

Of these, two will be remembered as long as men live in Ireland. The first was concerning the lineage of his old friend King Aedan, who had continued to offer support to all that he did. One day, through a gift of the Shining Ones, Maedoc saw a vision of all the members of Aedan's family, from the beginning of his line to the end, who would rule in Ireland for generations to come. Maedoc wrote them all down in a verse that is still known to this day. Part of it says the following:

> *Supreme rule for a time to them,*
> *Three of them ruling over Ireland,*
> *Thrice three over the province of Connaught.*

> *Thrice five kings of them afterwards,*
> *Will succeed—I remember their names:*
> *Three Fergals, three Aeds,*
> *Three Nials, many Ualgargs,*
> *Tigernan, Amlaib, two Arts*
> *Five Conchobars, two Cathals*
> *and more . . .*

> *The kings who will succeed them,*
> *Till the end of the world,*
> *The name of each one will I relate . . .*

...

In every case it came about as Maedoc foretold, and in after years because of this he became known as a keeper of ancestral wisdom. But the third great vision that is told of him concerns not so much his own seeing as that of another who saw him do a most wondrous thing.

It happened that Maedoc had gone to a high place to commune with the Shining Ones and the Spirits of the great ones of Ireland. Though he knew it not, a child followed him and lay hidden in some bushes, watching. And so it came about that this child saw a golden ladder descend from the heavens, and watched as Maedoc climbed it until he could no longer be seen. Long hours the child lay and watched and wondered, until at last, Maedoc returned by the way he had gone, climbing down the golden ladder, which then vanished from sight. The child could keep silent no longer but burst forth from his hiding place to demand where Maedoc had been.

"I will tell you if you promise never to speak of what you have seen while I live," said Maedoc. And when the child gave his word, Maedoc told him how he had been told that the spirit of the great Colmcille has departed from life, and because he wished very much to take leave of this wise and holy man, he had been granted permission by the Shining Ones to visit and speak with his spirit. As he had promised, the child never spoke of this until after Maedoc's death, when he was himself in the fullness of his years and gave an account of it, to the wonder of all who heard.

Not long after, Maedoc heard that he was to die within the year and that he should prepare himself accordingly. He did so, visiting all the communities he had founded and entrusting their continuance to those who shared his vision. To each one he left relics: a bell to one, a staff to another, a book to a third. And then finally he returned to Rossinver and there died. But even after death, his wonders continued. A man who had lain sick for almost thirty years had a dream in which he saw a chariot containing a man and a woman. When he asked who they were, the man revealed that he was Maedoc and that the woman was no less than Brighid, and that they had come to bless him. The man recovered sufficiently to speak of this and then died peacefully. So for long years after, Maedoc was remembered and his vision kept alive among the Celli Dé and those who sought to drink of their wisdom.

Maedoc's life is one of deep vision and overlaps, to an unusual degree, with that of an older, pre-Christian society. His visionary abilities are such that one is reminded, again and again, of the old Celtic shamans, who like him had an understanding of the world of the spirits that enabled them to better experience the world about them. Maedoc's relationship with the land is profound. It enables him to make a fair pathway

through a shifting bog, and (in an incident not included in this retelling) to walk on water. When he seeks to raise the body of the drowned youth, the waters of the lake give up their burden gladly. This act alone not only emulates the abilities of other great teachers to bring the dead back but recalls the way in which the older shamans could identify the dead from a single bone. Daimin seems to recognize Maedoc, having, we assume, encountered him in his wanderings in the realm of the spirits. This knowledge seems to aid Maedoc in recovering the lost youth.

Indeed, if there is one single theme in the golden skein that is Maedoc's life, it is his connection with the ancestors. His birth is foretold by the great Irish hero Fionn mac Cumhail, in a poem that bears all the hallmarks of being genuinely old (perhaps adapted from another older character to fit that of Maedoc). And of course, he makes a great and extraordinary prophecy (extending to many more verses in the original) that gives an account of the entire lineage of Aedan, whose appearance he so dramatically changes.

This episode seems more reminiscent of pre-Christian magic than the work of a saint and recalls a character known as Avagdu, or Utter Darkness, in Welsh mythology. This youth was so ugly that no one would have anything to do with him, until his mother, skilled in magic herself, sought not to transform his face but to give him wisdom instead, so that those who spurned his appearance would at least gain from his knowledge. It might be said that Maedoc acted unwisely in altering the king's appearance, which, after all, followed a natural course of events, but he shows his deeper wisdom in looking beyond this to the good that will come of it. Aedan not only (according to Maedoc's own prophecy) sired a long line of kings but also continues to support Maedoc in his work of creating monastic foundations, through which he is enabled to share his wisdom more widely.

Of all the episodes in Maedoc's remarkable life, it must be the one in which he is observed climbing a golden ladder to commune with the spirit of the recently dead Colmcille that marks him out as above the ordinary, and as a true inheritor of the Celtic shamanic tradition. As already noted, the practice of climbing the pole of a tent, or of a mighty tree, was a symbolic act that the tribal shamans of old Europe undertook to give a visual aspect to their inner, spiritual journey. In fact, as they climbed, they went into a light trance, which enabled them to travel out of the body and enter the realm of the spirit, where they received information relevant to the tribe whose spiritual welfare they oversaw. What, if anything, Maedoc learned from Colmcille is not recorded, but we may be sure that from the conversation of two such wise and holy men, only something of a powerfully mystical nature could emerge.

In many ways, perhaps Maedoc's life seems more remote than that of some of his brethren, but in fact all of us are far more deeply connected to the realm of the ancestors than we realize. Modern shamanic practitioners, who apply the techniques of soul work and healing to contemporary ailments, would recognize the importance of Maedoc's links with the "great dead" as a means not only of maintaining links with the cultural history of the Celts, but also of accessing knowledge and wisdom from the past that might otherwise be lost.

Travel between the physical realm and that of the spirit was a commonly understood and widely practiced event at the time in which the Celtic saints lived (roughly between the second and ninth centuries CE). It was considered by no means strange or unlikely for one person to apply to the ancestors, living or dead, for advice—and in many parts of the world to this day, it is normal to pray to the spirit of one's grandparents or great-grandparents for help in time of trouble.

For us today as individuals, no matter where we live, ancestral links can reconnect us with the heritage of our own family and the native culture from which we originate. Many contemporary forms of illness have been traced back to events in the chain of the family life that have not been fully or even partly recognized. Such fundamental problems as child abuse, incest, and the breakdown of the family can be seen as originating in the ancestral past, and by accessing and exploring such unhealed wounds, these can be dealt with effectively. Even the simple act of admitting a slight or injury toward some member of your family, either now or in the past, can have an immensely healing effect. At a deeper level, it may be necessary to forgive wounds dealt by ancestors who are no longer living, an act that can have a profound effect on the individual at a soul level. Unresolved conflicts can fester as deeply as any physical wound, and the acknowledgment of such—often hidden—agendas, now or in the past, releases us to continue living our own lives. By considering our own relationship to parents, life partners, and children—even those members of the family who are no longer alive, we find that things that have interrupted the flow of our own soul's journey can be healed and removed.

That Maedoc's experience reflects this shows up again and again in the story given here—his connection with the deep inner places of the soul, where matters of ancestral import are so often found to be the key, is what makes his story so important to our own continuing journey.

MEDITATION POINTS

- What is your own relationship to your family?
- How aware are you of your cultural and ancestral roots?
- Are there unresolved differences in your family's past?
- How can you deal with these?
- Do they affect your own life today?
- Are there people to whom you should say sorry, either now or in the past?
- Are there ancestors of whom you are aware who have had a profound effect on your life?

Recollections

God help my thought
That strays from me always;
I fear danger from it
On the day of judgment.

Through all the ways it goes,
Often down the wrong road;
Shouting, rushing,
Quarrelling even before God.

Through thrusting throngs,
Through troops of women,
Though woods and cities,
Faster than the wind!

Now by straight paths,
Now by rough;
Harsh ways, easy ways,
I do not lie!

Wandering, it crosses seas
Without a ship;
Leaping in a single bound
From earth to heaven.

Unwisely running
Close and far,
After every excursion
It returns home.

I've tried to bind it
To fetter its feet;
But it's still not constant
Nor mindful to rest.

Sword and lash,
cannot restrain it;
As slippery as an eel
It eludes my grasp.

Neither lock nor prison,
Chain nor earth,
Fortress or sea
Will hold it fast.

Dear Christ, to whom
All is clear,
May a sevenfold grace
Keep and control it.

Govern my heart
Stern God of the Elements;
May we be together
In your enduring fire.

(Tenth-century Irish; J.M. after Kuno Meyer)

...

TWELVE

THE HOSPITALITY OF THE HEART

BERACH OF CONNAUGHT
(February 15)

Berach the sweet-lipped
Left disbelieving brothers
Hospitality of a true lord . . .
—Betha Berach

...

We know less about this saint than about almost any of the ones gathered together in this book. The text of his life, the Betha Berach, was, according to the colophon of the text, "copied from a bad old vellum book, belonging to the children of Brian O'Mulconry the younger . . . on Feb 6, 1629, by the poor friar Michael O'Cleary." On the evidence of the text itself, Berach was born at Gort na Luachra (the Close of the Rushes) near Cluain Conmaicne in Connaught. He seems to have been roughly contemporary to Kevin of Glendalough, though he was some years younger since the foundation there was already functioning by the time he arrived. This puts him as alive in the sixth century. He is patron saint of Kilbarry in county Dublin. Beyond this, we have no further information other than that contained in the text of his life, which remains one of the most quietly powerful accounts of the Celli Dé that I have found.

Berach's miraculous encounters with warriors mark one of the key themes in his story, as does his long quarrel with the poet Dairmait, which has a ring of historical truth about it. Berach is able, through the power of his faith, to transcend the petty squabbles of other men, and his actions at the battle of Cluain Coirpthe mark him out as a figure with powers every bit as effective as those of the Druids, who were performing similar feats only a few years earlier. Among the many half-

forgotten tales of the Celtic saints, Berach's deserves to be better known; it's hoped that its inclusion here will bring it out into the light of day again after many years of obscurity.

In the Field of the Sun

When Patrick was bishop over all of Ireland, he went into Connaught and visited the house of Dobtha, the son of Aengus. They gave Patrick a great welcome, and Dobtha's wife told him to go and catch some game for the table. Dobtha and his sons went out at once and had better luck than ever before. When they returned, it was almost dark, and though the entire household searched high and low, they could not find so much as a single lamp or candle to light the house. Then it is said that Patrick worked a great miracle, for he called back the sun so that it shone briefly again over the land of Ireland. For which reason the spot where this took place is called Achad Greine, the Field of the Sun.

Now the cauldron was set above the fire, and Dobtha and his wife and sons and Patrick and his clerks gathered about it. And Patrick spoke the words of blessing upon the house and talked of the Great Mystery, so that Dobtha was moved to ask for baptism. But Patrick shook his head. "I will not baptize you, for a child shall be born to you and your wife, and of its line shall come another who will bring that gift to you himself. And I promise you further," he said, "that you shall not die until that child is grown and shall come to you with the blessing of God." Then the great saint made a further prophecy, which was that when the child of whom he spoke returned to that place, he would build a great foundation on a nearby stretch of boggy ground. "That is a hard place to build," said Dobtha. And Patrick, with a flash of his eyes, answered, "What is hard for man is easy for God." Then he promised a gift to the child, that he should have the hospitality of the heart from all good men, and that each one should contribute a burning brand from their fires to his fire, and that he himself would contribute a brand from his own fire. Neither Dobtha nor his wife understood this promise at that time, but in days to come they would remember it and see how great the foresight of Patrick was.

The Bright Years

And so Dobtha lived on in the Field of the Sun, and his wife bore him three sons, one of whom, Nemhall, took a wife named Finmaith, who bore him a son whom they called Fintan. Many signs and wonders surrounded his birth, and before long all knew that he must be the wondrous child of which Patrick had foretold. So, he was given into the care of a man named Fraech to foster, and he, in turn, gave the child a new name, Berach, which means acute or sharp, for the clarity and sharpness of his wits was so great that all came to honor him for his wisdom even before he became a man.

When he was only seven years of age, Berach went to study with the great Daigh, son of Cairell, who was noted for his wisdom and the depths of his teaching. And there, one time, came some distinguished guests. But all the household members were away save for Daigh and Berach, so the youth washed the feet of the guests and then went to prepare supper for them. He found that there was only a small sack of wheat in the storehouse, and even this needed to be ground before it could be used. Berach hurried at once to a nearby mill and begged the woman he found there to grind his wheat before the oats that she was about to grind. Not only did the woman refuse, but she spoke harshly to Berach and slightingly of his master. At which, Berach emptied his bag of wheat into the mill, and to the amazement and fear of the woman, the mill wheel ground out wheat meal from one side and oatmeal from the other, without mixing them at all!

At that moment, the woman's husband and sons arrived and, hearing what had happened, threatened to kill Berach. But when he looked at them their weapons stuck to their hands, and they could not move at all until they begged his forgiveness and promised him no harm. Then Berach took his sack of milled wheat and went home.

Berach and Kevin

When he heard of these events, Daigh said that Berach should no longer remain in his house but should go at once to Glendaloch, where Kevin would be his new teacher. Then he gave him a gift, a small bell that had great powers, having belonged to another holy teacher in the past. So Berach set out across Magh Murthemne and by way of the river Boyne into Bregha. Along the way he passed through the lands of the king of Tara, who was preparing a feast for another king. Berach asked for a drink and was refused. "Well," he said to the steward, who had turned him away. "The feast would not have been the less for the sake of one drink." Then he went on his way. But that night when the feast began, it was discovered that the fifty vats of beer that had been set aside for the occasion were all bone dry—though they had been full earlier. "Who has been near them?" demanded the king. The steward remembered Berach as the only other person apart from himself who had been near the vats. "Go after him," said the king. "But do not harm him. Ask him to return here and eat with us and be sure to ask him politely."

The steward went after Berach and soon overtook him. Red-faced, he begged the youth to return, and Berach did so. When he entered the hall, he drew forth the little bell that Daigh had given him, and rang it once. Its sweet chimes filled the hall, and at once the vats were filled with the finest beer ever drunk in that place. Then the king asked for Berach's blessing and received it, and afterward he sent many provisions to feed both Berach and his growing followers in time to come.

Then Berach went on his way and soon arrived at Glendalough, where Kevin welcomed him warmly. But Berach saw that his host was troubled, and when he asked the reason he learned that Kevin's cook had but lately died. Now he had guests and no one to prepare food for them. "Let me do it," asked Berach.

In the kitchen he found scant food and drink, but what there was, he gathered on a great table. Then he divided the amounts exactly into two halves, one at each end of the table. Then he blessed each amount, and they became twice as much as before. Three times again he divided the food, and each time there was double the amount when he had blessed it. Then he prepared as fine a meal as had ever been eaten in Glendalough. When Kevin learned what had happened—knowing full well that there was little provender in the kitchen—he gave thanks to Berach and begged him to remain there for as long as he wished.

Faelan the Fosterling

Now Kevin had a beloved fosterling, Faelan, the son of Colman, who was himself son to the king of Leinster. A frail child, he was often heard crying for things he needed. One day he was crying out for milk, and at that time Kevin had none to offer him. When Berach heard this, he raised a hand and blessed the mountain before him. Then he said, "Let the doe that is upon this mountain come hither." And the doe came and gave its milk for Faelan.

On another occasion, Faelan was crying out for the healing plant called sorrel. This was hard for Kevin since it was the winter, and no sorrel grew at that time. But when Berach heard this, he put his hand upon a certain rock, and at once sorrel sprang up through it and covered it. Many say that this rock is still there, and that sorrel grows upon it out of season every year because of the miracle of Berach.

Yet again when Berach himself was with Faelan, the child cried out for apples. Berach looked around and saw only a willow tree growing nearby. "God can do even that," he said, and he put his hand upon the trunk of the tree. At once a heavy crop of apples was upon the willow, and Berach plucked some and gave them to Faelan.

All these things were done because Faelen was a child of special promise who would one day himself be a leader and teacher of men. But he had a stepmother named Caineach, who had married the king of Leinster after his first wife, Kaelan's mother, had died. Now she had sons of her own, and when she heard of the wonders wrought for her stepson by Berach, she became fearful that he would displace her own children. Therefore, she gathered about her a number of women of power and came to Glendalough with the intention of harming the boy. One of the Shining Ones came to Kevin and told him of this, and Kevin in turn told it to Berach to see what he would do.

At once, Berach set out to meet the women. He came upon them at the top of a mountain and there addressed them, asking them to return home and to leave Faelen in peace. At this, Caineach raised her hands to lay a curse upon Berach, but he merely raised a hand against her and her companions and said, "Be under the earth." At once the earth opened and took them within the body of the mountain, after which they were seen no more.

The Battle of Cluain Coirpthe

For a few years more, Berach remained in Glendalough, until Kevin said that he should go forth and make his own way in the world. "For it is time that you fulfilled the prophecy of the blessed Patrick," said Kevin. Then he had all of Berach's things placed in a chariot and summoned a stag to pull it. "Wherever this stag shall stop, there shall I remain and build my foundation," said Berach. Then he set forth with his attendant Maelmothlach and some others who wished to go with him from Glendalough. Many days they traveled, until at last the stag came to the edge of a wide plain, and there it stopped and lay down. "This is the place where we shall stay," said Berach, and he sent Maelmothlach to explore the area.

Very soon the attendant returned with grim tidings. It seemed that a battle had been fought in the fields that very day, and a great slaughter made. "This is a terrible place," said Maelmothlach. "A place of death and corruption." Berach opened his eyes very wide and looked away into the distance. "It shall be called the Meadow of Corruption," he said, "lest anyone forget it." Then he went forth onto the field and found there a fort over which the battle had been fought. And when he had stood and contemplated it for a time and walked among the dead and dying who lay upon the field, Berach began to work a wonder of the greatest kind. Circling the field, he chanted aloud and blessed all who were there. And where he walked, men rose up that had been dead, and stood blinking in the sunlight. And at the center of the field, he came upon the bodies of the two princes who had fought there. They were Donnchad of Tara and Tipraite, son of Tadg from Cruachan. These two also Berach healed, and to Tipraite he gave back life. And he made peace between them.

Afterward a poet among the hosts made a song of the battle, which said,

Donnchad and Tipraite,
Both their great forces
Fell in the wide enclosure,
At the centre of the fort;
Every mantle was torn
Every shirt bloody
Every wound inflicted.
Until there came
Berach of the fair face
And woke the sleepers
From the place of death.

...

Then the two princes made peace and went their ways, leaving Berach to begin the work of clearing the land and building upon it. And soon, when the work was completed, came Berach's old foster father Fraech, and his teacher Daigh, and they blessed and consecrated the foundation. Also it was at this time that Berach journeyed to the place where his grandfather, Dobtha, now greatly aged, was still living. There, just as Patrick had foretold, the old man received the sacrament of baptism from the hand of his grandson, and soon after he died peacefully and was laid to rest in the graveyard of the monastery.

The Poet's Challenge

But Berach's tenure in that land was not to be easy, for there lived at that time in the same place a poet named Diarmait, who was mighty in both song and druidcraft. He had made a song praising Aedh, the king of Connacht, and the king had rewarded him with the gift of land, which included the place upon which Berach had begun to build. When he heard this, Diarmait grew angry and sent word to Berach to leave. Berach refused, saying that Patrick himself had chosen this spot for him and had prophesied that he would occupy it.

The two men met under a certain thorn tree at Rathonn, which was sacred to Dairmait, to discuss the matter. But they could not agree, and so they went before King Aedh and asked for a judgment. But secretly, Diarmait told the king that if he chose in favor of Berach he would satirize him in such a way as to raise boils on his face. The king knew that this was no idle threat, for such was the power of poets in those times. He also he feared Berach for the miracles he had performed. Therefore he refused to give judgment in the matter.

Berach and Diarmait searched the length and breadth of Ireland for someone who would give a judgment for them, but they found no one who would do so.

"Let us go to Alba, to the land of the Scots," said Diarmait, "for there we shall certainly find one wise enough to settle this heavy matter."

Berach agreed. They went first to the fort of Aedan mac Gabran, one of the high chieftains of Scotland in that time. It happened that there was a great feast about to happen, so that many young warriors were out in the meadows below the walls of the fort trying their hand at various sports. Diarmait hurried ahead of Berach and spoke to them. "An impostor is coming," he said. "Attack him with cudgels and dung and stones." And, because Dairmait was finely dressed and Berach only in a simple robe, the warriors believed the poet and hurried to attack Berach. When he saw them coming, he held up a hand and said, "May you be unable to do what you intend." At once, all the young men stopped still as if frozen and could not move a muscle.

Dairmait glowered at this and hastened on. Soon the two men stood before the gates of the fort, and Dairmait pointed to two mounds of snow that stood on either side of the entrance. "If you were any kind of a holy man, you would make fire of that snow so that we could warm ourselves." "Let fire be made of them," said Berach. "Go and blow on them, O poet." And Dairmait went and blew upon the snow, and it burst into flame. Then he was silent.

Meanwhile these deeds had been noted by the servants of King Aedan, who asked his Druids what manner of man this visitor was. The Druids went into the inner place where visions are found and returned with knowledge that they gave to the king in verse.

There is no noble shining saint
Who could attain such deeds
Save Berach the triumphant
From fair Rathonn

Berach, son of Nemhall
Son of Nemargen of heroic strength
Is no landless man,
His power is mighty
When he puts it forth.

His swiftness is revealed,
He turns away evil,
Bright gold his breast
As the morning sun.

•••

When he heard this, the king ordered that Berach and Dairmait be admitted to him, and he honored them both. To Berach he offered land in Scotland to found another monastery, and this Berach promised to do, leaving behind some of his followers to begin the work. Then both he and Dairmait laid their grievance before the king, who after a time gave as his opinion that only one man was wise enough to make a judgment in the matter of the land, and that was Aedh, the son of Brennain, the king of Tethba.

So Berach and Dairmait the poet returned again to Ireland and went to Tethba and asked the king for a judgment. And the king declared that an assembly should take place at Lis Ard Abla—that is, "the High Fort of the Apple Tree"—to discuss the matter. But when they came there, and many other of the Celli Dé and the high lords of Ireland also to hear the judgment, Dairmait began to revile Berach because they were not meeting beneath the thorn tree at Rathonn, which, being a sacred spot to him, he thought the only place where they might speak together without anger. And Berach looked at Dairmait and said, "Then let the thorn tree be brought hither." And in a moment, to the wonder and terror of all who were present, and most especially to Dairmait, the tree was carried through the air and settled in the earth beside them.

When he saw this, the king declared that he could make no judgment, since a higher authority than his had already made itself known. This only made Dairmait angrier than before, and he rose to make a satire upon Aedh. Then Berach stepped forward and placed a hand over the poet's mouth. "Neither satire nor praise song shall pass your lips until the day you die. And that I declare shall be within a year."

At this, Dairmait could no longer hold out against the power of Berach, and he bowed his head and departed. When he was gone, the thorn tree once again lifted itself into the air and went back to Rathonn, where it is said it may still be seen to this day. And Berach gave thanks to the king of Tethba, and, having released the young warriors, who had remained unmoving all this while, he returned home. Soon after, Dairmait left the land for which he had fought, though he continued to live nearby and, whenever he could, lost no chance to revile the name of Berach. But in all that time he was unable to compose a poem, either a satire or a praise song.

And so the days passed until it was almost a year since the day of the assembly, and Dairmait was heard to say with a sneer that Berach's prophecy was not going to come true.

But later that day, as the evening was drawing in, there came a great commotion outside Dairmait's house, and he went to look out. There he saw a group of hunters, who had cornered a stag just below his window. Even as he stood there, one of the huntsmen flung a spear, which missed the stag but struck Dairmait instead, killing him outright.

Thus was Berach's prophecy proven true, but the matter did not end there. For Dairmait had a son named Cuallaid, and when he heard of the manner of his father's death, he rose up in the spirit of vengeance to curse Berach and the land over which the poet and the wise man had fought. He set out with nine others to curse Rathonn, so that no corn would grow there and the cows refuse to give milk, and the trees in the woods remain leafless.

When Berach heard of this, he sent a trusted attendant, who was named Concenn, to challenge Cuallaid and his followers before they could do any damage. "See that you offer them no harm," ordered Berach. But Concenn did not do as his master had bidden. He was a wild-tempered youth, and when he saw the poet's son coming along the road in his chariot, he hid in some bushes, and when the chariot drew near he threw a spear that struck Cuallaid on the head and felled him to the earth.

Concenn fled when he saw the result of his actions, while Cuallaid, who felt his death approaching, ordered his men to carry him to a certain hill from which he might overlook Rathonn and curse it still. But when he came to the top of the hill, he was too weak to stand and, with his failing sight, could see only a single clump of oak trees. These he cursed with his last breath, and ever after they would bear no fruit or leaves but stood as though dead.

Then Cuallaid's men went to Berach and begged his forgiveness, and he was much saddened by Concenn's actions and spoke of his regret for all that had happened through the quarrel over the land.

With the matter thus ended, Berach worked hard to bring his vision into being. Many people came from all parts of the land to hear him speak, and many brought brands of light and understanding from the fires of their hearts, so that the words of Patrick long ago, that Berach should have a flame from the fires of many men, was finally understood. And ever were Berach's words of forgiveness, and of the hospitality of the heart that all men should have toward each other.

Berach lived to a great age and performed many more miracles that are recorded in the books of the Celli Dé. But one remains that must be told here, since it speaks so well of the great wisdom possessed by Berach.

Once there was a famine in Ireland, and many went short of even a crust to feed themselves. In the lands adjacent to Rathonn lived a man named Laegachan, whose wife went heavy with child. One day, Laegachan went out in search of food, and he said to the woman before he departed that if she bore the child while he was away, she should kill it, for they had nothing with which to feed it. And not long after he was gone, the woman bore the child indeed, and it was a boy. The woman could not bear to kill it but devised a plan to save its life by taking it to Berach, for she knew that he would not refuse to care for it. So she gave the babe to one of her women, who went to Rathonn and told Berach what had occurred. When he heard this, he wept openly. Then he said, "Take the child back to its mother. Assure her that the means to feed it shall be found."

So the woman returned home with the child, and as she entered the house there came a great noise outside. Everyone rushed forth to see what had caused this, but they could see nothing. This happened twice more, and on the third time they saw an otter dragging a mighty salmon, the largest anyone there could remember seeing, toward the house. When it saw the people, it ran off, and they pulled the huge fish inside and cooked and ate it. And there was sufficient meat on the fish to last them several months, by which time the famine had passed. Later, when the child was grown to manhood, he came to Berach and served him faithfully until the time of his death.

On the day long appointed, one of the Shining Ones came to Berach and told him that his time was come to pass out of the mortal world. And it is said that Berach went willingly and with a smile on his lips, leaving behind a great foundation where the wisdom he had taught was remembered and shared with all who came there for many generations afterward.

The story of Berach is only a small step away from the great mythic stories of Ireland. Though he is a wise and holy man, Berach's powers extend far beyond those normally attributed to the Celli Dé. In the episode of the Battle of Cluain Coirpthe, for example, he is able to raise the dead to life again and thus to end the conflict that might otherwise have brought a shadow upon the land where he intended to build. Later we read of Cuallaid's curse, which is recognized as real enough to blast a clump of oaks, though the land about them is spared. Such curses are common throughout the heroic literature of the age, but it is rare to come across it in the life of a saint.

Berach's long-standing feud with the poet Dairmait has a ring of authenticity about it. According to the complex laws of the time, Dairmait probably had every right to be where he wanted to be, but the earlier prophecy of Patrick is seen to take precedence over that of the king's gift. Their long search for a judgment shows how delicately the balance was between pagan and Christian communities in the Celtic world, as well as illustrating of the power possessed by the poets at that time. In order of precedence, a poet ranked only third in importance to the king himself, and such were their powers that it was widely believed that a satire could actually have physical results, such as the raising of boils on the face. This was called a glam-dichenn, and one of the most celebrated is described in an ancient text known as Cormac's Glossary. Here the satirist is the famous bard Nede, who makes a satire against King Caier that is recorded as being as follows:

Evil, death and a short life to Caier;
May spears of battle slay Caier;
The rejected of the land and the earth is Caier;
Beneath the mound of the rocks be Caier.

...

Next morning, when the unfortunate king went to wash, he found that three discolorations had appeared on his face—one crimson, one green, and one white—signifying disgrace, blemish, and defect. Since the law of the time stated that no king bearing a disfigurement of any kind could rule, Caier was forced to flee and Nede became king in his place.

While the struggle between Berach and Dairmait never goes this far, it is a serious matter for all that, and Berach's final prohibition, that no poem or songs should come from the mouth of his enemy, is a terrible one indeed.

The two central themes of Berach's life revolve around justice and blessing. We see him overcome opposition by recourse to the law, as in the case of Dairmait, or as in the instance of the warring warriors at the battle of Cluain Coirpthe, he brings justice to them by working through what we might call "natural" law. This same theme comes out again in the whole matter of the judgment before King Aedan, who in the end refused to cast his vote either way, since a power greater than his has already decided. In our own lives we see this happen again and again, in cases where we think we have the right, or see that another is in the wrong, only to have circumstances change the direction of our thinking.

The blessings that Berach offers are manifold and range from the miracles he performs for the child Faelan to the way that he is able to defend himself from unworthy attacks by simply blessing the space before him or the people in question. Thus he brings the doe from the mountain to feed Faelan and stills the warriors of King Aedan by the simple raising of a hand. Indeed, most of his miracles draw upon the natural world in one form or another, and like so many of the Celli Dé, his relationship to the animal kingdom is important, such as when he calls the otter to bring the huge salmon to feed the starving family.

But perhaps the most wonderful image in the story is the prophecy of Patrick and its eventual fulfillment. Patrick promises that Berach's fire will be fed with brands from many fires, and this is indeed so. His own light is a single flame, but from the flames that grow independently around him, a greater fire is created. We can learn from this the importance of combining and sharing our individual flames, which together make something more than we could ever produce on our own. Others can take fire from our example as we live our lives to the best of our abilities. Berach offered the hospitality of the heart to all who came to him. In our own lives the magic of the heart fire will be perceived by others as a warmth and inner strength that draws them to us naturally as friends and coworkers. If you know someone in your life who is like this, a gentle being around whom others constellate, then he or she is more than a little like Berach.

MEDITATION POINTS

- What is the spark of divine fire in you, and how does it manifest?

- How strong is your sense of justice?

- Consider an event in your life in which you feel you were unjustly treated, and ask yourself how this came about.

- See past your personal point of view to the point of view of others.

- Look about you and try to find someone who naturally draws others to them by the light of their inner fire.

- Is there poetry in your life, and, if not, how can you manifest it there?

God of the Moon

God of the moon, God of the sun,
God of the world, God of the stars,
God of the waters, the land, and the skies,
Who ordained for us the King of Promise?

It was Mary fair who went upon her knee,
It was the King of Life who went upon her lap,
Darkness and tears were set behind,
And the star of guidance rose early.

Illumined the land, illumined the world,
Illumined both doldrum and current,
Grief was laid and joy raised up
Music was played on bright harp strings.

(The Carmina Gadelica)

...

THIRTEEN

THE DEER'S CRY

PATRICK OF ARMAGH
(March 17)

Come hither, Patrick, hither come!
Shield of the Gael, thou light of story
Appointed star of golden glory!
(Anonymous; translated by Robin Flower)

...

Patrick is something of an enigma. Despite his fame, the details of his life are so contradictory that it is hard to get a really accurate picture at all. He is famed as the first and greatest bishop of Ireland, but he may well have been self-appointed and never to have actually been consecrated in this office at all (indeed, there is some doubt whether he was even a monk). He is famed as the patron saint of Ireland, but he was born in Britain of Welsh and Breton parents. He is the only one of the Celli Dé who left a partial account of his own life—the Confessions—which has been so often misquoted and edited that few would now recognize the original. Yet, for all this he remains a shining light among the stories of the Celtic saints, and his inclusion in any collection such as the present one is inevitable.

Even Patrick's dates are doubtful, though most authorities now place his birth at around 390 and his death at ca. 461 CE. His father was a decurio (town councilor) and also a deacon in the local church. His mother, whose name may have been Concess, remains a dim figure in the background.

They lived in a town named Bannaven Taburniae, in the area of Strathclyde. Captured by pirates while still in his teens, he returned to Britain and was trained in the rudiments of Latin theology (he later bemoaned the fact that he had not received a better education). Returning to Ireland in ca. 435, he established a base at Armagh, which has continued to claim him as its patron ever since.

Doubt overhangs Patrick's death as it does much of his life. The fact that the exact place of his burial remains unknown has enabled several rival churches to lay claim to his relics. Glastonbury in Somerset, famous for its connections with the Arthurian and Holy Grail legends, claims that he came there for a time—though in fact it was probably another Patrick who did so. Eight early churches and foundations in Britain and another three in Wales are named after him and claim connections with his life. He is the primary patron of Ireland, and in our own time his feast day, on March 17, has become something of a major holiday, especially in the USA and Australia, where families of Irish descent have made his day their own. The main cathedral in New York City is dedicated to Patrick and organizes the great parade that throngs the streets of the city every March.

His legendary struggle with the pagans of Ireland may not be all it seems, since as with much of his legend, it has been rewritten to suit the needs and wishes of later generations. It is far more likely that Patrick felt a certain affinity with the Druids he is generally depicted as fighting, while his own powers, as with several of his fellows, are equal in every way to those of his adversaries and every bit as magical.

Patrick's life is, like that of his fellows, full of wonder and miracles. But there is another Patrick who lingers beneath the more colorful aspects of his legendary self. It is that of a sincere and essentially simple man, whose generosity of spirit so impressed his contemporaries that they treated him as a saint virtually within his own lifetime. The story he tells in his own words confirms him as both likeable and honest, a seeker after truth whose example still shines out to all who are dedicated to the soul's continuing journey today.

Even before birth, Patrick wrought a wonder. His father was Calpurnius, of the Strathclyde Britons, and his mother was Concess, daughter of Ochmass, who hailed originally from Lesser Britain. In the early days of her pregnancy, Concess entertained a certain king, washing his feet and giving him wine to drink and bread to eat. The king was moved by her beauty and looked with longing upon her, so that his wife, the queen, became eaten by jealousy. Secretly, she prepared poison and gave it to Concess in a drink. But the child, waking in the womb, seized the dark draft and turned it into a stone. When Concess in time gave birth to a healthy son, he was born holding the stone in his hand.

Near to the place where he was born lived a wild youth named Gornias, who was blind. He had a great reputation as a seer and wise man, and Patrick's mother wished to take her son to be blessed by him. When they reached the cave, Gornias came forth to meet them, clad in skins. He turned his blind eyes toward the child and blessed it. Then he said, "This child will outreach all others in this land. His name shall be remembered throughout Ireland and beyond." Then he turned away and spoke no more, though it is said by some that he regained the sight of his eyes thereafter.

When it came time for Patrick to be fostered, as was the custom in those days, he went to live with his mother's sister, who was barren. One day, as winter loosed its grip upon the land, there was a great flood that came into the house where they lived. The heath fire was quenched, and all the vessels and gear of the house were afloat in the water. Seeing this, Patrick cried out that he was hungry and began to weep. His foster mother reproached him, saying, "How shall we make food without a fire? We have troubles enough without this!"

Then Patrick stopped crying, and a light came into his eyes. He gathered some dry straw and, standing on a dry place, dipped a hand into the water. Five drops ran from his finger ends, and as they fell, they became sparks of fire. The straw caught and blazed up, and Patrick fed the flames with tinder and flakes of wood. The water came no higher, and while the child laughed in delight, his foster mother watched in wonder.

Nor was this the only time that Patrick showed himself master of fire. Another time, his foster mother asked him to fetch faggots for the hearth fire. Patrick went forth and returned with handfuls of icicles gathered from the doorsill. The woman scolded him, saying, "These will not warm us!" But Patrick answered, "If we only believe it, these icicles will flame like withered wood." And as he said this, he threw the ice into the fire, and it blazed up at once.

Not long after this, it happened that some children in the village where Patrick dwelled brought fresh honey to their mothers; all save Patrick, who returned empty-handed. "Why do you not bring me honey?" said his foster mother. Without a word, Patrick rose and took a vessel and went outside to the well. Filling the jar with water, he blessed it and brought it back inside, where it was found to be filled with the finest honey imaginable.

After this, his foster mother sought to test him. It happened that a woman who used to work alongside her in the milking sheds had a child who died. As she mourned, Patrick's foster mother told her to bring the dead infant to the milking place and to lay it in the straw alongside the cattle. Then the two women began to milk the cows. In a while, Patrick came there, and his foster mother gave him a foaming jug of milk to drink. "Call that other boy to share the milk," she said and watched to see what Patrick would do. Without hesitation, he called to the dead boy. "Come, share my drink." The dead child awoke and rose up and came to him and was fulfilled. The women were filled with wonder and knew that the prophecy made by Gornias had already begun to be true.

Capture and Restitution

When Patrick was little more than thirteen years of age, he traveled to Brittany with his parents to visit his mother's family. It so happened that four sons of the king of Britain had been exiled to that land, and out of anger and frustration they ravaged the town and villages in the area. In the fighting that followed, both Calpurnius and Concess were killed, and Patrick, together with his sisters Lupait and Tigris, were captured and taken by ship to Ireland, where they were sold into slavery to different masters.

Now there followed a period of seven years during which time Patrick grew to manhood and served his master so well that he received nothing but praise. Miliuc was his master's name, and he was king over Dalriada, a harsh yet not unjust man. Yet, though he suffered no more than the loss of freedom, Patrick's heart yearned for his homeland, and he continued to mourn the deaths of his parents and the loss of his sisters.

Patrick's chief task was herding and caring for his master's large herd of sheep, and this often placed him alone in the wilder part of the lands over which Miliuc ruled, especially to the woods of Fochlad. There it was that he began to discover a part of himself that he had hitherto been only half aware. The wonders he had performed as a child had passed him by; he scarcely remembered them as more than dreams. Now he began to sense the world around him to be full of a wonderful energy of which he himself was a part. Day after day, as he sat watching over the sheep, he began to walk deeper and deeper into the secret places of his soul, and there it was that he encountered a presence that, though it had neither face nor name, he came to recognize as other, separate from himself. Soon it spoke to him, teaching him the ways of wonder, enriching his life and deepening his awareness of the living world.

At length, a time came when Patrick could no longer remain silent with all the thoughts that were within him, and he began to speak of what he had learned, at first only to his fellow thralls, then to the children of his master, who, having heard him speak, returned to listen to his words.

So the time passed, until it was the seventh year of his captivity, at which time, as was the custom, a bondsman might be set free. Miliuc, who grew daily more conscious of the value of his slave, took thought as to how he might keep him longer. To this end, he purchased a bondswoman, whom he gave in marriage to Patrick on condition that he remained in service for a further seven years. When he saw the woman, Patrick noticed a white scar on her brow. "How came you by that mark?" he asked. "It was when I was but a child," the woman answered. "I fell and struck my head upon a rock. My brother, who possesses the skill of healing, laid his hand upon me and I was restored." Then Patrick wept, for this was indeed his own sister, Lupiat, who had been carried off into slavery with him.

The next day as he watched over the sheep, the inner voice spoke to him, saying, "The vessel is prepared for you. Drink and set forth, for the world has need of you."

"I shall not go without my master's leave," replied Patrick, and the voice was silent.

So Patrick went to Miliuc and asked his leave to depart.

"You may go, but you must pay me a gold piece for your freedom." replied his master.

Then Patrick returned to the wild lands and spoke with the inner voice, telling it what he must do to earn his freedom. "Tomorrow, when you return this way, a boar will come this way," said the voice. "Watch how it digs in the earth. It will turn up the treasure you require."

Patrick did as he was bidden, and sure enough, when the boar dug in the earth it turned up gold enough to purchase not only his own freedom but that of his sister. So the two left that place and set out for Britain. There Patrick was joyously received, and as the people became acquainted with his wisdom, they begged him to stay there and to teach. But Patrick found that his heart was restless, and the inner voice spoke to him of far-off lands and the learning that he might find there. So he took a ship to Gaul and there found his way to the foundation of the great Germanus, who instructed him in many wondrous things and encouraged the gift that was within him to grow and flourish. But ever it seemed to Patrick that he heard the voices of the children he used to teach in the woods of Fochlad calling out to him: "We beg you, holy boy, to walk among us again!"

Return and Resistance

So it was that Patrick set out again to return to Ireland. But this time he came in triumph, and of his own free will. And when he was close to the mainland, he saw a little island rise from the sea close to his ship. On it were two people, a man and a woman, who seemed aged beyond the years of mortal men.

"Who are you?" cried Patrick.

"We have been here time out of mind," said they. "We await the coming of one who will set us free."

"I am that one," said Patrick, for his inner voice told him this was so.

Then the ancient ones wept and gave to him a staff carved with intricate designs. "This shall be your sign," they said. "Take it with our blessing." And Patrick took the staff and went on toward the land.

He landed at the place that is nowadays called Inispatrick, from where he went to stay in the house of a worthy man named Sescnech. This man had a young son who, when he saw Patrick, was so enchanted by him that he would not leave his side. That night he would not sleep with his father or mother but chose instead to lie on a pallet next to Patrick. In the morning, he clung to the visitor and would not be parted from him. When he saw this, Patrick blessed the child and bade him wait until he might come and be with him for as long as he wished. "For this shall be the first of my followers," he said, and indeed in time to come the child, whose name was Benen, became his foremost attendant and remained with Patrick until the day of his death.

Once word got out that a new and wise teacher had come into the land, people came from all over to hear him, and soon Patrick had a large following. Then he set out to visit the king of that part of Ireland, a fierce warrior named Loeguire, son of Niall, to ask permission to teach and build in his lands.

It so happened that Patrick came to Tara of Bregh, where the king held court, on the eve of Loeguire's feast day, at which time he had given forth a decree that no other fire might be lit in all the land until he had lit the fire of celebration in Tara. Patrick, ignorant of this edict, kindled a blaze on the Hill of Fiacc, and there he celebrated the Mysteries of Christ.

When word of this came to Loeguire, and he saw for himself the pinpoint of fire on the distant hill, he was greatly angered. "Who dares to defy me in my own land?" he demanded. And one of his Druids, overhearing this, quoted to him a prophecy that had been made three years earlier:

> *The Adzeheads will come over a furious sea,*
> *Their mantles over their heads,*
> *Their staves crook-headed,*
> *Their tables in the east of their houses.*
> *All who hear them will answer: Amen.*

...

"This is one of those who were prophesied," said the Druid. "They will destroy you and all your kingdom if they are permitted to remain. Also, unless this fire is put out tonight, it will continue to burn for a thousand years."

Then Loeguire was troubled indeed and summoned his war band and his chief Druid, Lucetmael, and they set forth at once to confront Patrick. He, when he saw a forest of torches and a glittering of spearheads coming toward him across the plain of Tara, went to meet them.

"Who are you that dares to light a fire in my land on this night?" demanded Loeguire.

"I am called Patrick. I seek to teach and build schools in this land."

"You shall not do so while I am king," declared Loeguire. Then suddenly he gave a signal, and his war band advanced.

When he saw this, Patrick called upon the power that lay within him and raised the staff he had been given by the undying folk of the island. At once a cloud of absolute darkness descended upon the king's men, and the earth shook beneath their feet so violently that they began to flee, stumbling and falling upon each other in the impenetrable gloom.

Then Loeguire cried out, "Let us talk!," and at once the shaking ceased and the darkness retreated. Then the king called for wine and bade Patrick sit down with him. But as the cup was passed from one to another, the Druid Lucetmael spat into it. When the cup came to Patrick, he blessed it and the liquid at once turned to ice. Then he upended the cup, and a single drop of spittle fell out, the very same that Lucetmael had put in. Patrick blessed the cup once more, and the wine became liquid again.

Then Lucetmael rubbed his hands and said, "Let us work wonders on this great plain."

"What kind of wonders?" demanded Patrick.

"Let us bring snow over all the land," said the Druid.

"I shall not do anything that is contrary to the law of God," answered Patrick.

The Druid then began to work his magic, and in a while, snow lay over all the plain, a foot deep, so that all marveled.

Patrick looked at the snow and said, "Very well. Now take it away again."

"That I may not do," said the Druid, "until morning."

"It seems you can manage only half a task," said Patrick, and as he spoke the snow began to melt away, until the plain was clear again.

Then the Druid summoned a darkness of his own, but Patrick dispelled that.

Things might have continued in this way for much longer, but at last the king himself declared that both should undertake a test to see who was the strongest. The test was to be an ordeal of fire, and both agreed to attempt it. Loeguire called upon his men to build two huts, one made of green wood and the other of dry wood. Then he declared that Patrick should go into the dry hut and the Druid into the green hut. This they did, and the huts were set on fire. The green hut in which the Druid sat was consumed, and he with it, but the hut made of tinder dry wood in which Patrick sat would not even catch fire at all.

When he saw this, the king acknowledged that Patrick was a man set apart, a veritable Druid, and swore that he would trouble him no more, but that he might be allowed to teach and go wherever he liked. Secretly, however, he planned to lay a trap, and to kill Patrick and all who followed him.

Next morning, Patrick and his followers set out to cross the plain of Tara. As they came to a place where rocks lay tumbled about the earth, the inner voice that always went with him spoke to Patrick and warned him that Loeguire and his men lay in wait for them. Then Patrick summoned up all his strength and made a great invocation, which may still be heard on the lips of men to this day. Thus he spoke:

I gird myself today
With the strength of God,
With God's might to uphold me
God's wisdom to guide me,
God's eye to look before me,
God's ear to hear for me,
God's words to speak for me,
God's hand to guard me,
God's way to lie before me,
God's shield to protect me,
God's host to save me,
From all who might harm me,
Both near and far,
One or many . . .

...

As he spoke these words, Patrick and his companions took upon them the appearance of deer and thus passed through the ambush without harm. From which cause to this day the invocation of protection is known as "the Deer's Cry."

Death of a Legend

After this, King Loeguire troubled Patrick no more but allowed him to go where he would and to do what he wished unchecked. And so, the word of this great new teacher began to spread throughout Ireland until there was scarcely any place where his name was not known and his deeds not celebrated. Wherever he went, he taught the wisdom he had earned in the wilderness and built foundation and schools where the word of God might be spread abroad.

In Armagh he built a great church, and ever afterward the people of that place claimed him for their own. But it was not intended that Patrick should die there, or for his bones to lie where any man might discover them. For when he was old beyond the years of most men and felt his death come near, he set out for Armagh, being at that time in the county of Derry. But the voice that had spoken within his soul so often before reproved him, asking why he undertook this last journey without its guidance. Then it told him that he should remain where he was until the hour when his soul must leave his body. Then the voice told him, "Let two wild oxen be set free to wander upon the road, and, wherever they stop, let that be the place of your burial."

"It seems," said Patrick with a sigh, "that I have ever been in thrall." But he gave instructions that all should be done as the voice had told him, just as he had always done, and when the moment of his death came, it is said that a great light shone around his body for two nights. Afterward, the oxen were released as Patrick had requested, and they stopped at a crossroads midway between the lands of Derry and Ulster. There Patrick was buried, though in later times it is said that his bones were taken from there to another place. It is wisely said that he, whose name shone like a star over all of Ireland, should remain hidden in the land, so that no place may claim him for its own.

Patrick is a man under orders. Right from the start, when he is recognized by the strange blind youth Gornias, he is set apart, and later, when he becomes a slave, he begins to learn about the hidden depth of the spirit under the guidance of an inner voice. He emerges from the state of imprisonment—which is metaphorically of the soul as well as the body—with new insights and ever-deepening wisdom. Not only is he a wise and powerful teacher, but a natural magician also, one of whom the term "shaman" could very fairly be used. This may seem at odds with the more usual portrait of Patrick, but every incident told in the foregoing story is recorded in one or other of the lives that tell of him.

The truth or otherwise of these is not in dispute; that he was perceived in this way by those who followed him is an indication of the person he really was. Episodes like the one in which he conjures fire from water (five drops: a significant number to the ancient Celts) or receives the gift of his staff from the undying people on the island—an episode that might have come from any one of a hundred otherworld adventures of more-ancient heroes—point to his unusual nature.

Patrick had always been represented as a hero, a soldier of God who faces the unfriendly kings of Ireland with their wonder-working Druids and wins; who brings the dead back to life and calls the elements to serve him at will. The extraordinary way in which he escapes from the trap set for him by changing himself and his companions into the shape of deer is both a measure of his mature power and an interesting reflection of a more ancient practice. The Dear's Cry recalls a druidic method of shape-shifting called the Fith-Fath (pronounced "fee-faw"), in which the person who wished to become invisible recites a charm and takes on the shape of a beast. Patrick, as in the earliest instances in his life, uses druidic magic for his own protection, invoking his God in the same way as his forefathers would have invoked theirs. To this day, people make prayers of this kind, which are often called a "lorica" or "breastplate," to invoke protection against all kinds of dangers. The ancient poem that follows below is a striking combination of pagan and Christian imagery, as powerful a plea to the universe as Patrick himself might well have uttered.

The very striking ordeal by fire that he undertakes as part of his struggle with the Druid Lucetmael is also part of an older tradition that is recorded in a text known as The Irish Ordeals. In this, a number of tests and trials are listed:

Mochta's Adze. It was put over a fire of blackthorn until red hot, then passed over the tongue of the person suspected of falsehood. If it burned, the person was guilty; if not, the suspect would be freed.

•••

Sencha's Lot-Casting. Lots were cast out of a fire. If the accused were guilty, they cleft to his palm; if not, they would fall to the earth. Sencha used to make a poet's incantation over them.

•••

The Vessel of Badurn. Badurn was a king, whose wife had entered a faery mound and obtained a magical crystal cauldron that, if three untruths were uttered in its presence, would burst asunder. Then, if three truths were uttered, it would reassemble itself.

•••

The Three Dark Stones. Three stones—one white, one black, and one speckled—were put into a bucket filled with black stuff from a bog. If the accused were guilty, he would bring out the black stone; if innocent, the white; if only partially guilty, the speckled.

•••

The Cauldron of Truth. This was a vessel of silver in which water was heated to boiling point. The accused then put in his or her hand and, if scalded, was deemed guilty; if not, innocent.

•••

Luchta's Iron. A sacred iron that Luchta the Druid brought back from Brittany. It was heated and put into the hand of the accused. As in later medieval tests, if the iron burned them, the accused was deemed guilty; if not, innocent.

•••

Waiting at an Altar. In this ordeal the accused had to go nine times around the altar before drinking a cup of water over which an incantation had been chanted. If he or she were guilty, their guilt became manifest upon them. We are not told how this happened, but presumably either the guilty one fell dead or was forced to speak the truth.

•••

What Patrick's ordeal is telling us is that he cannot be killed, because he still has work to do—indeed, his work is really beginning from here on, and as he blazes a trail across Ireland with his inspired teachings, his response to the needs of the people who enslaved him—the Irish—whose voices he hears calling out to him, is to "walk again in or land."

The invisible bond between himself and his former captors is teased out by divine inspiration, leading him to return to Ireland. We do not know if those who came to hear him knew of his own story and past status as a slave. If they did, they would have been impressed by his courage in coming back to serve the land where he had been held captive, for they loved above all to hear stories of heroism, especially those where failure, sorrow, and difficulty caused the hero to persist in impossible service.

Patrick's complaint of "always being in thrall" is a complaint that arises in even the most committed individual—there is never enough "personal time or space" for those who are dedicated to spiritual service as Patrick was. How we can find ways of reinventing our work, of refreshing it and reinspiring it with meaning, is something his story can show us. We need to take time out, to be quiet and contemplative, without the stimulus of books, music, or TV—to come again into the forgotten country of the soul. We need to spend time "in the wilderness," learning the old truths that are still there within us but may have been forgotten in the rush to succeed, to endure the pressures of life. Watching Patrick's growth into his own spiritual journey, from the carefree wonders of his childhood to the sustained and conscious acts of his later years, is a journey we must all follow, and from which we can learn every time we stop to consider it.

MEDITATION NOTES

- When did you last make time for inner work in your life?
- Consider what you can do to improve your ration of personal time.
- What kind of things inspire or motivate you to make greater efforts?
- Ask yourself if you are in service to anything outside your ordinary daily activities.
- Try creating your own lorica or breastplate, for use in moments of doubt and fear.

Lorica

I invoke the seven daughters of Ocean
Who weave the threads of the sons of age.
Three deaths be taken from me,
Three lifetimes be given me,
Seven waves of surety be granted me.
No illusions disturb my journey,
In brilliant breastplate without hurt.
My honor shall not be bound by oblivion.
Welcome age! Death shall not corrupt the old.

I invoke the Silver One, undying and deathless,
May my life be enduring as white bronze!
May my double be killed!
May my rights be upheld!
May my strength be increased!
May my grave not be dug!
May death not visit me!
May my journey be fulfilled!
I shall not be devoured by the headless adder,
Nor by the heard green tick,
Nor by the headless beetle.
I shall not be injured by a bevy of women
Nor a gang of armed men.
May the King of the Universe stretch time for me!

I invoke Senach of the seven aeons,
Fostered by faery women on nurturing breasts.
May my seven candles never be extinguished!
I am an indestructible fortress,
I am an unassailable rock,
I am a precious jewel,
I am the prosperity of the weak.
May I live a hundred times a hundred years,
Each century in turn,
The fullness of their brew my sufficiency!
The encircling of the Spirit's fortress be about me!

(Anonymous, eighth century;
translated by Caitlín Matthews)
...

FOURTEEN

THE WELL AND THE SALMON

KENTIGERN OF SCOTLAND
(January 14)

Power of wind be thine
Power of sun be thine
Power of water be thine
Power of earth be thine.
—Gaelic incantation

...

Historically, little is known about St. Kentigern, beyond the fact that he was probably born toward the end of the sixth century CE, that he was a bishop, and that he spent most of his life bringing Christianity to the Celtic tribes in the area of Strathclyde. Yet, traditions concerning his life abound, including two versions of his life and several fragments that together build into a rounded portrait of an extraordinary man whose ability to see into the heart of things gave him prophetic powers and the gift of healing. His story is often considered to be connected with the life of the famous poet and prophet Myrddin, better known to us as Merlin, the archetypal wizard of King Arthur's court. There may, indeed, be some truth in this, since Kentigern was almost certainly contemporary of both Myrddin and the historical Arthur. Lailoken, the wildman who may have been Merlin, suffers the same threefold death as the great enchanter—a death generally given only to Druids or people of power.

According to widely held tradition, Kentigern (whose name means "Hound-Son of the King") was believed to be the illegitimate son of Urien of Rheged, a semihistorical figure in his own right who turns up again in the romantic stories of Arthur as a king and warrior and is present also in the early history of Merlin. The same sources relate that Kentigern studied with Servanus, a sixth-century Scottish bishop whose own life is as vague as his pupil's but who may have been the apostle to the Orkney Islands.

Having created a foundation in the Strathclyde area, Kentigern is said to have run into difficulties with the local leaders and to have been exiled to Cumbria (or possibly North Wales), where he founded a monastery said to have numbered nearly a thousand monks. Later he returned to Scotland and lived at Hoddam in Dumfries and at Glasgow, the city that has claimed him as its own and contains his relics in its cathedral of St. Mungo (an alternative name for Kentigern). He is believed to have died in 612, possibly aged eighty-five—though this too may be apocryphal. Many of the people and places mentioned in the story are real—Rederech was a real king who ruled over part of Strathclyde in the sixth century, while Kings Morken and Caswallen are both known historical personages.

Whatever the truth about the life of this passionate and extraordinary man, his life offers a picture of magical and wondrous events, from which—especially in the episode of the healing of the wildman Lailoken, or the many elemental aspects of his life—we may draw patterns of healing and vision for our own lives.

In the dark days after the departure of the Legions, King Loth ruled over much of northern Britain. A proud, harsh-natured man, he had one daughter, Tanau, whom he prized above all things. This girl had a simple heart, and when she found herself to be with child, though no man had known her, she believed that one of the Shining Ones had come to her and given her the gift of a baby. But when the king learned of her state, his anger knew no bounds, and when neither threats nor cajoling would persuade her to give up the name of the man responsible, Loth, raging, insisted that she be given over to the justices, to suffer the harsh penalty meted out to unmarried women found to be with child—that she be taken to a high point and flung down to her death.

Tanau bore all the slights and torments of her captors with fortitude, believing herself chosen to bear a wondrous child, and only when she was taken to the summit of the hill called Terapain Law did she utter a prayer that if her own life was not to be spared, then at least that of her unborn child might be. However, her pleas fell upon deaf ears, and she was placed in a chariot, and her hands bound to its rails. Then, at a signal from the judges, the chariot was pushed off the top of the hill.

The chariot should have fallen and smashed both itself and the body of Tanau on the rocks below, but instead—wonder of wonders!—it touched the earth as lightly as a feather, and the bonds that held the king's daughter fell away as though they had never been. Tanau stepped away from the chariot without so much as a scratch upon her, while those who had gathered to watch her execution stood amazed.

When Loth heard what had happened, his anger was even greater. He gave it as his belief that his daughter's escape was due to some evil magic. And though many people thought that he should have taken note of the wonder that had befallen and set Tanau free, instead he decreed that she be subjected to a further ordeal—to be placed in a coracle and set adrift in the open sea. "If she be worthy of life," he declared, "her God will save her."

Thus Tanau was taken to the mouth of the river named Aberlessic and placed in a small skin boat without oars or rudder. This in turn was set upon the outgoing tide, which soon carried it from the shore. And many there noticed a strange thing. The mouth of the river had long been known as a place where fish were to be found in great numbers; yet, when the coracle bearing Tanau was carried out to see, the fish followed it as though escorting the craft, and ever afterward it was said that the waters thereabouts remained unproductive of fish.

For three days and three nights, the frail craft was carried on the backs of the waves, with Tenau huddled in the bottom. In all that time she never once cried aloud with fear or doubt, being sustained by an inner sense that all would be well for her and the child she carried. Thus, the morning of the fourth day dawned, and the coracle was cast up on the shores of Cullenross. Weakened by lack of food and water, Tenau crawled ashore and fell into an exhausted sleep. There she was discovered by some sailors, who, seeing that she was near to her time, carried her to their own shelter and cared for her until she gave birth to a boy of great beauty and sweetness.

Then, consulting among themselves, and having heard something of her story, they decided to take her to the wise teacher Servanus, who was at that time living nearby. When he saw Tanau and the child she bore in her arms, he saw the light that shone from both mother and child, and took them in. "For," said the wise and holy man, "I believe there is a great future for this small one." The child he baptized forthwith, giving him the name of Kentigern, which means Hound-Son of the King, though whether he came by this name through vision or by other chance I cannot say.

Child of Wonder

Tanau and her child were given into the keeping of certain holy women, and when the child reached an age where he might be instructed in matters of the spirit and the world, Servanus himself took upon him Kentigern's education, finding in him a willing and able pupil who soon showed himself as remarkable as the wise teacher's perception had shown. Many stories are told of these early days and give witness to the youth's wondrous nature.

At that time, there were some ten other youths who studied with Servanus. Kentigern was not popular with any of his fellow pupils, who perceived him as a favorite of their master. Thus, they ever schemed to do him ill and, behind the back of their teacher, bullied and tormented him in any way they could. In spite of which, Kentigern retained a sunny temperament and spoke no harsh words against his companions.

Now Servanus had a tame bird, a robin, that came to him every day and in many ways exhibited its love for him. On one occasion the students captured this bird and began to make sport of it. However, it happened that the bird was injured, and in its terror it fell dead. The pupils, fearful of the anger they knew that Servanus would visit on them, sought to blame Kentigern, who had in fact taken no part in their cruel sport. When he saw what had occurred, he took the dead bird in his hands and sought to warm it with his breath, praying over it with closed eyes. To the wonder and fearfulness of Kentigern's school fellows, the bird's heart began to beat again, and it flew from his hands to see its beloved master.

After this, the youths hated Kentigern even more and gave thought to how they could bring him into disrepute. Now it was his task to see that the rush lamps in the little church where Servanus gave blessing and teaching to the people in the area be kept alight, and he invariably rose early in the morning to see that wicks were trimmed and oil replenished. One day the other pupils woke even earlier and crept into the church to douse all the lights. When Kentigern came later, he found the building cold and dark, with no fire from which to take a light. Concerned, he wandered out into the predawn stillness and found himself by a stream, on the banks of which grew a hazel bush. As he looked upon it, a light was kindled in its heart, and, filled with wonder, he drew forth a single branch, which at once burst into flame between his hands. Joyfully, Kentigern bore the light back to the church and lit all the lamps, at which point the branch ceased to burn. Afterward he planted the hazel bough close by, and it is said that in time it grew into a stand of hazel trees that always had a light about them, as though warmed by an inner glow.

The Way Ahead

After this, the other pupils hated Kentigern more than ever and strove to make his tenure with Sevanus daily less pleasant. Finally, after several more months of this, Kentigern looked within and found the vision to depart the place. Not wishing to bring hurt to his old tutor, he left secretly, at night, and followed a wandering path until he reached the banks of a swift-flowing river. There, as he hesitated over which path to take next, the waters were divided, and there before him stood one of the Shining Ones, beckoning him across.

Filled with wonder, Kentigern crossed the river dry-shod, and thereafter the river flowed back and rose so high that it burst its banks and spread over the land on either side, making it impassable to all. But as Kentigern stood and watched all this, he saw the bowed figure of Servanus approaching the farther side.

"Would you go without even taking your leave?" Servanus called sadly.

"I sought only to give you less pain," answered Kentigern.

"Have you forgotten everything that has been between us?" said Servanus. "How you came to me as a child, and how you have learned from me ever since. Indeed, I am more father to you than any other living man."

"It grieves me to leave you," said Kentigern with tears in his eyes. "But the time has come for me to seek out my destined way. These waters that are between us are a token of this. Neither of us may cross it, and I must go my way and you yours. But do not think that I love you any the less because of this. I know now that I have always awaited this moment, and that the time has come for me to follow the path ordained for me."

Then Servanus wept openly. "It is as you say, and I know this also. Nevertheless, my heart is heavy. Go with God, my son, for I see that the way is clear before you."

Servanus turned away and went back to the school where he had lived and taught for so long. Soon after, he died, some said of a heart broken by the departure of his beloved son Kentigern.

Kentigern the Bishop

For a while now, Kentigern pursued a wandering way. In time this brought his steps to the place called Glasgow, and to the door of a house, within which he found a man close to death. When the man saw Kentigern, he called out his name, then told him that a vision had told him that a man bearing his name and face would come, and that only when he had received Kentigern's blessing could he die. Much moved by this, the youth blessed the sick man, who died forthwith with a smile on his lips.

Kentigern saw this as a sign that he was destined to remain in Glasgow, and since the sick man had gifted him with all his worldly possessions, he had the wherewithal to begin creating his own place. In the next year, he began to build a church and outbuildings to house those who would soon come to study with him. Stories of his miraculous powers and spirituality spread quickly through the northern lands.

It was said that when he celebrated the mysteries, a light often shone out from him, and that on occasion a white dove flew down and settled on his shoulder. Wherever he went, he read the mysteries of the elements, speaking of the beauty of air, fire, earth, and water. Another time when he needed to plough a field and had no cattle, he called upon two mighty stags and harnessed them to his plough. Later, one of the stags was attacked and killed by a wolf, and when Kentigern saw this, he called upon the wolf to submit itself to him. This it did, and to the wonder of all, Kentigern harnessed the remaining stag and the wolf together, causing them to pull the plough in harmony.

It was this act alone that caused the people of Glasgow to ask Kentigern to be their bishop, and despite his protests that he was still too young, they would not accept his refusal. Soon after, at the age of twenty-five, he was duly consecrated and began at once to pursue his ministry with sincerity and devotion, seeing to the building of churches and the foundation of several new monastic settlements.

So, for a time all was well with Kentigern, and word of his wisdom spread throughout the land. But soon after, the old king died and a new leader, named Morken, took his place. This man was powerful and greedy and had no love for the Celli Dé. Thus he took to speaking ill of Kentigern, calling him a sorcerer and an evil magician and imputing his works. For a time, Kentigern was able to ignore this, but matters came to a head when, seeking provender for his numerous and widespread followers, he approached the new king with a request for grain.

"I have none to spare," declared Morken, whose barns were in fact bursting. "And even if I had, I would never give any to you."

But Kentigern persisted gently, explaining his needs in greater detail, until at length the king shouted at him to leave. "If your wisdom is so great, see if you can move the contents of my barns to your own place without my help. If you can perform such a miracle, you may have anything you can get!"

Quietly, Kentigern took his leave and returned to the settlement at a place named Mellindenor, on the river Clud. There he spent time in prayer and meditation. Soon after this, the river began unexpectedly to rise. In the city where King Morken held sway, it burst its banks and, islanding the royal grain store, lifted the barns from the earth and bore them away, depositing them finally at Mellindenor, where Kentigern gave thanks and dispensed the grain—miraculously dry despite its journey by water—to those who needed it.

After this, King Morken felt only hatred toward the wise bishop, and on an occasion soon after when Kentigern had occasion to visit the royal palace, Morken became so enraged that he kicked out with his foot and laid the bishop on the earth. Kentigern himself made no complaint, despite the anger of many of his followers. But soon after this, Morken's foot began to swell with gout, and in less than a year he was dead.

Many saw this as a judgment upon him for his insult to the holy bishop, and though Kentigern himself offered prayers for the dead man's soul, Morken's family was filled with hatred for the bishop and sought for ways to destroy him. Twice attempts were made on his life, and in the end, at the insistence of his followers, Kentigern departed from Glasgow and fled into Wales, where he was made welcome by the blessed David. Here also, the king, Caswallen by name, made it known that he rejoiced to have Kentigern on his lands and offered him lands on which to found a new community.

Kentigern, joyful in this news, traveled to the lands offered to him. There, accompanied by a number of his most devoted followers, he wandered through the lands, seeking a sign where he should begin to build his new foundation. And there, as they walked near a grove of trees, came a great white boar, which circled them for a time and then finally came and laid its head on the earth before Kentigern. He, touching its bright, wicked tusks, followed where it led, to a sheltered place in a thickly wooded valley. "Here," he said, "we shall build." And he blessed the boar, which at once ran off into the tress and was seen no more.

So, work began at a pace, with trees felled and foundations dug. Then came the local prince of that land, Galganau by name, who demanded to know by what right Kentigern should build there. Even the name of King Caswallen had no effect upon this proud man's heart, and he ordered his soldiers to burn down all that Kentigern and his followers had built. But as he rode away, Galganau was struck by a sudden blindness, and in fear he was brought back to the bishop, who stroked his brow as he had stroked the white boar's tusks, at which the prince's sight was restored.

After this, there was no further opposition to the work of Kentigern and his followers, and in a while the foundation began to grow and flourish, with people coming from far and near to stay there and to listen to the inspired teachings of Bishop Kentigern.

For a time, the foundation had no name, but it acquired one in remarkable circumstances. Kentigern was given to meditation and prayer in the open air, sometimes sitting for hours together, unmoving and unconcerned by the weather. On one occasion the air was so bitterly cold that the holy man virtually froze. It was thus that one of his youngest followers, a boy named Asaph, found him. When the youth saw that his master could scarcely move for the cold, he ran back to the monastery and, hastening within, took two hot coals from the fire and hastened back with them in either hand to where Kentigern sat. With the coals he made a fire, and slowly Kentigern was freed from the spell of the cold. As for Asaph, his flesh was not at all burned by the carrying of the hot coals, and when Kentigern heard of this wonder, he declared that the foundation was to be named after Asaph. Many years later the boy would himself become the leader of the community, and longer still after that, it is known still as St. Asaph's.

The Ring and the Salmon

After this, Kentigern remained in Wales for a number of years, growing wiser and more beloved every day. At the end of that time, he received word that a new king, Rederech, now held power in the northern lands, and that this king desired greatly that Kentigern return to his old place at Glasgow. And, since the foundation of

Asaph was well established, Kentigern agreed, and having made Asaph himself the foundation's new leader, he set off back to his native lands. There he received a tumultuous greeting from the people, and both the king and his queen, Langoreth, came forth to welcome Kentigern.

Not long after this, there occurred an incident that is listed among the greatest of the wonders performed by Kentigern. The queen had fallen in love with a young soldier in her husband's guard and, in a moment of foolishness, gave to him a ring that the king had given her. The soldier, proud of this love gift, took to wearing the ring, and it was not long before another of the king's servants saw and recognized it. Immediately he went to Rederech and told him of this evidence of the queen's infidelity.

At first, the king was reluctant to believe this talebearer, but when he saw the ring he became, first of all, suspicious and finally convinced. As soon as he could he organized a hunting trip and took the soldier along with him. There, as the young man slept under a tree, Rederech took the ring and threw it into a nearby river. Then, on his return, he asked the queen, in seeming innocence, where the ring was that he had given her.

Turning pale, Langoreth said that she would search for it, that she believed it put away in one of her jewel boxes, and at once she sent a secret message to the soldier to return her ring. When he confessed that it was missing, the queen knew that she was doomed and threw herself upon the king's mercy.

Rederech was unmoved and demanded that his queen be taken into custody and tried for treason and adultery. It was only as she languished in her prison cell that Langoreth thought of Kentigern. She sent a message begging him to come, and in due course the now-aging bishop arrived. The queen confessed her guilt and begged him for help, promising never to give way to such foolishness again. And Kentigern, who saw that in her heart she still loved the king, and remembering perhaps his own mother's punishment for transgressing the laws of men, promised to do what he could.

Returning home, he instructed a messenger to go to the nearby river and there to cast in a line and bring to him the first fish he caught. The man obeyed and soon returned with a large salmon. Kentigern took a knife and, opening up the fish, withdrew the very ring that the king had thrown into the water. This he sent secretly to the queen, who at once summoned her husband and showed him the ring. With this evidence, Rederech was forced to pardon his wife, and in truth he was well deposed to do so, for he too still loved the queen and had feared to see her punished.

Only long years after, when King Rederech was dead, did the queen tell of Kentigern's part in the affair, and it was counted among the many wonders that he performed in the twilight of his life.

The Bishop and the Wildman

One of the last of these concerned a strange wildman called Lailoken, whom some believe to have been a name adopted by no less a figure than the seer Merlin, whom madness had taken after he witnessed the terrible carnage at the Battle of Arderydd. It happened that Kentigern used to walk often in the quiet of the woods near his home, listening to the songs of the birds and the murmur of water from a spring that rose in the depths of the forest, which was believed to possess healing properties. But one day when he approached this place, he found that another was there before him—a strange figure clad in skins with long and matted hair and beard. He looked at Kentigern with wild, blank eyes and then ran shrieking into the trees.

After that, he was often there when Kentigern came to the spring, and though at first he always ran off, in time the presence of the bishop no longer seemed to worry him. Indeed, when Kentigern made no attempt to communicate with him, the wildman gradually began to look for his coming and finally learned to sit with him, absorbed in the tranquility of the spot.

At last, one day he spoke, in an old, cracked voice, rusty from lack of use.

"What are you?" he asked.

"A man, just like you," answered Kentigern.

But the wildman only shook his head at this and ran off.

Next day, however, he returned, and Kentigern was able to speak with him again, gently encouraging him to reveal more of his nature. Eventually the wildman's story was pieced together. How he could no longer stand to be in the world of men after seeing his fellows slain in battle. Now he lived in the forest, his only companions the trees and the wild animals whose society he sought in preference to that of men.

As the two men spoke more, Kentigern learned that the wildman called himself Lailoken, and that he had a gift for prophecy that was perhaps part of his madness. Many things he told the bishop as they sat together listening to the voice of the water. Then, one day, Kentigern asked the wildman if he wished to be healed, and to live among his own kind again.

"At times I grow weary of birdsong and beast grunt," Lailoken said.

"Then drink from the wellspring, for I believe it can heal you."

Slowly, Lailoken looked at the water welling forth, then at the face of his companion. Slowly he put his hands into the water and cupped them and brought water to his mouth. As he drank, his eyes became clear again, and he looked with wonder at his surroundings and at his own wild state.

Gently, Kentigern took him by the hand and led him back to his own home. There the wildman remained for a time, as his spirit slowly returned to him. But though healed in body and mind, he retained the gift of prophecy—though it was ever after a wild and uncertain gift, which led him to speak often in words that few could understand. Indeed, his hold on reason was slender, and at times he would revert to his old wild ways—though he never again strayed far from Kentigern, who seemed much like a father to him.

Years after, when Kentigern was celebrating the mystery of the Eucharist, Lailoken sent word that he was shortly to die. He asked for a blessing from the holy bishop and also sent a strange message.

"I shall die today in three ways: for I shall be stoned, pierced, and drowned."

When he heard this, Kentigern and all those with him shivered, for such triple deaths were not unknown in those days and always presaged the passing of a great one.

Kentigern sent his blessing to his old friend and heard later that he had indeed met his end as he had prophesied, for some servants of a man whom Lailoken had offended, by telling him of his wife's infidelity, set upon him and stoned him. Struck repeatedly, the wildman fell over a steep bank of the river, where a sharp branch pierced his body. As he fell back dying, his head went beneath the water, and he drowned. Thus was Lailoken's last prophecy fulfilled, and in token of the friendship that had been between them, Kentigern saw to it that he was laid to rest beneath the trees of the forest, close by the spring where they had so often talked.

Not long after this, Kentigern himself, now of great age and venerability, died. His last words to those who gathered at his bedside were to remember the wisdom of the wild things, to trust the baptism of the elements, and always to honor the healing power of the waters. Many said that he was the greatest of the Celli Dé, and that his life was an example of the way that men should follow who would learn the wisdom of the great creation.

Kentigern's life contains many riddles that, if we look at them open-eyed, we can begin to understand. From the beginning, his life is affected by the four primary elements of earth, air, fire, and water. His mother suffers two punishments, that of air (by falling down from the high place) and water (by her journey at the mercy of the sea). Kentigern himself, like so many of his fellows, is constantly in touch with the natural world in this way. He brings to life the dead bird beloved of his master by breathing the breath of life into it; he shows his command of the element of fire by lighting the candles in the church from the branch that bursts into flame at his wish; he heals the mad Lailoken through water; he is linked to the earth through animals—as when he is led to the site of his future monastic settlement by a white boar, an animal ever held sacred by the Celts—and recovers the lost ring from the

body of a fish (to this day, Kentigern's insignia are a salmon and a ring). In addition, he suffers a near death from cold (another elemental challenge) and is released by his novice Asaph, who is able to carry hot coals to warm him without suffering harm.

It may well be that behind the story of Kentigern lies a far-older tradition, concerning an ancient solar hero. His mysterious birth (watched over by shepherds) is reminiscent of that of more than one wonder child, including Christ, the Roman Mithras, and the Middle Eastern Attis. Each episode in his life has to do with an element in one way or another, and these are clearly Kentigern's link with the infinite life of the spirit. His soul's journey is through contact with the presence of the divine in the elemental world, and through this he is able to bring healing as well as wisdom to those in need.

Among the Celts the elements were always perceived as doorways into an infinite universe. Fire was the fire of inspiration and brought the other elements in its train. The ancient and semimythical Irish poet Amairgin expressed it thus:

> I am a wind on the sea,
> I am a wave on the ocean,
> I am the roar in the sea . . .
> I am a tear in the sun,
> I am a salmon in a pool . . .
> I am a god who fashions fire in the mind . . .
> (Trans J.M.)
>
> •••

Water was the way between the worlds, whether by way of the voyage that led out of this world, out of ordinary reality, into another place, or by imbibing the stuff of wonder and mystery from one of the many sacred cauldrons or wells that appear so often in the ancient Celtic tradition. Again and again, we find references in Celtic literature to the power of water to transform the individual, to act as a conductor for the most-profound mysteries. An ancient Gaelic prayer says, "May God give you to drink from the Cauldron that never runs dry," a reference to the many wondrous vessels of plenty and inspiration that are found scattered throughout Celtic tradition. Thus the sixth-century Welsh shaman-poet Taliesin imbibes universal wisdom from a cauldron in which has been brewed a distillation of all knowledge. Once he has drunk this, he goes through a series of transformations that take him through each of the elements: he turns into an animal, a fish, a bird, and a grain of parched wheat. Afterward he has the knowledge of each element, which instructs him in a better understanding of all created life.

We too can learn by observing and honoring the elements around us. Every day we breath air, warm ourselves by fire, bathe in water, and walk upon the earth; yet, we seldom if ever notice or acknowledge the divine presence within each of them.

Breath itself had always been seen as the purveyor of life, and for this reason perhaps the Celts perceived the winds as bringing either good or bad fortune in their wake. According to early tradition, there were twelve such winds, each one blowing from a different direction and given a different color, name, and attribute. Solanus, the wind that blew in January, brought plague and disease: Africus, which blew from the southeast, was especially good for the propagation of fruit; Saronicus, from the south, was deemed to bring a good harvest; and so on.

In our own lives, we seldom orient ourselves to the directions or recognize the elemental quality they each carry. The oldest known traditions of the West designate the cardinal points of the compass with an element. North is equated with earth; south with fire; east with water, and west with air. These qualities themselves bear other references to less abstract things: North has to do with strength and the things that sustain us, such as hearth and home, family and friends. South brings us closer to the fires of inspiration and the energies of life itself, through creativity and the imagination. East has to do with the emotions, with love and hate, sorrow and joy, and the freedom of tears. West brings us the gifts of the spirit and connects us to all living beings.

By learning to resonate with the directions in our own lives, we can learn from them just as Kentigern did. Through being aware of the power of the directions, and by acknowledging them every day, we can enter into a greater harmony with the universe around us—the final goal of all spiritual seekers. We may never bring back birds from the dead or learn to foretell the future, but we can come to terms with some of the tests that life daily offers us.

MEDITATION POINTS

- Consider how you relate to the four primary directions and the elements they represent.

- What is your relationship to the earth beneath your feet?

- What is your relationship to the sky above you?

- To the air you breath?

- To the water you drink or in which you cleanse yourself?

- How do you respond to the element of fire—as a lighted candle or a roaring coal fire?

- Over four days, try to be as fully aware of each element as possible, giving your attention to one on each successive day.

- Look within to see how they affect you, and when you have done so, honor them in whatever way seems best to you.

Calendar of the Birds

Birds of the world, bright without shame.
It is to welcome the sun again;
at the nones of January, whatever the hour,
a host consorts in the sheltering wood.

On the eight of the calends of eminent April
Flights of swallows make congregation;
a strand of exile their concealment
from the eighth of the calends of October.

On the feast of Rudan, runs the saying,
all their fetters are unlocked;
on the seventeenth of the calends of May,
unceasing cuckoos throng the wood.

In Tallaght the birds relent their
sung music on the July calends
for Mael Ruan, whom the Badbh took not:
the living pray on that woeful day.

On Ciaran's feast, son of the smith,
the barnacle goose flues over cold seas;
on Cyprian's feast, a great contention,
the brown stag bells from the red plains.

Three score thousand years of whiteness
is the term of the world, without doubt;
billows will burst across every airt
at the end of night, at the cry of birds.

Renewing is the melodious music
of birds to the King of the bright clouds,
their praise to the King of stars:
listen to the feathered choir afar!

(Fourteenth-century Irish;
translated by Caitlín Matthews)

...

SOURCES AND FURTHER READING

1: LIVES OF THE CELTIC SAINTS

Adamnan. *The Life of St. Columba*. Edited by William Reeves. Llanerch, Wales: Llanerch Enterprises, 1998.

Ailred. "The Life of St. Ninian." In *Two Celtic Saints*. Llanerch, Wales: Llanerch Enterprises, 1989.

Baring-Gould, S., and John Fisher. *Lives of the British Saints*. Edited by Derek Bryce. Llanerch, Wales: Llanerch Enterprises,1990.

Curtayne, Alice. *St. Brigit of Ireland*. New York: Sheed & Ward, 1954.

Head, Thomas, ed. *Medieval Hagiography*. Garland Reference Library of the Humanities. New York: Routledge, 1998.

Joceline. "The Life of St. Kentigern." In *Two Celtic Saints*. Llanerch, Wales: Llanerch Enterprises, 1989.

O'Domhnaill, Maghnas. *Betha Colaim Chille*. Edited by A. O'Kelleher and G. Schoepperle. Dublin, Ireland: Institute for Advanced Studies, 1994.

O'Mera, John. *The Voyage of St. Brendan*. Dublin, Ireland: Dolman, 1978 and 1997.

Plummer, Charles, ed. and trans. *Lives of Irish Saints*. 2 vols. Oxford: Oxford University Press, 1922.

Stokes, Whitley. *Lives of the Saints from the Book of Lismore*. Felinfach, Wales: Llanerch Enterprises, 1995.

Stokes, Whitley. *The Martyrology of Oengus the Culdee*. Dublin, Ireland: Institute for Advanced Studies, 1984.

2: FURTHER READING

Bamford, Christopher. *The Voice of the Eagle: Homily on the Prologue to the Gospel of St. John.* By John Scotus Eriugena. Hudson, NY: Lindisfarne, 1990.

Bamford, Christopher, and William Parker Marsh. *Celtic Christianity: Ecology & Holiness.* West Stockbridge, MA: Lindisfarne, 1986.

Borlase, William C. *The Age of the Saints: A Monograph of Early Christianity in Cornwall.* Felinfach, Wales: Llanerch Enterprises, 1995.

Carey, John. *King of Mysteries: Irish Religion Writings, 600–1200.* Dublin, Ireland: Four Courts, 1998.

Carmichael, Alexander. *Carmina Gadelica: Hymns & Incantations.* Edinburgh: Floris Books, 1992.

Chadwick, Nora K. *The Age of the Saints in the Celtic Church.* Oxford: Oxford University Press, 1961.

Clancy, Thomas Owen, and Gilbert Markus. *Iona: The Earliest Poetry of a Celtic Monastery.* Edinburgh University Press, 1995.

Clarke, Amanda. *Holy Wells of County Cork.* Cork, Ireland: Wildways, 2023.

Darcy, Mary Ryan. *The Saints of Ireland.* Cork and Dublin, Ireland: Mercier, 1974.

Davies, Oliver. *Celtic Christianity in Early Medieval Wales.* Cardiff: University of Wales Press, 1996.

Davies, Wendy. "The Myth of the Celtic Church." In *The Early Church in the West.* Edited by Nancy Edwards and Alan Lane. Oxbow Monographs. Oxford: Oxbow Books, 1992.

De Waal, Esther. *The Celtic Vision London.* London: Darton, Longman & Todd, 1988.

Farmer, David Hugh. *The Oxford Dictionary of Saints Oxford.* Oxford: Clarendon, 1978.

Gregory, Lady Augusta. *Book of Saints & Wonders.* London: Colin Smyth, 1971.

Henken, Elissa R. *Traditions of the Welsh Saints*. Cambridge, UK: D. S. Brewer, 1987.

Hyde, Douglas. *Legends of Saints and Sinners*. London: T. Fisher Unwin, 1896.

Irvine, John. *A Treasury of Irish Saints*. Dublin, Ireland: Dolmen, 1964.

Lehane, Brendan. *The Quest of Three Abbots*. Hudson, NY: Lindisfarne, 1994.

Low, Mary. *Celtic Christianity & Nature*. Edinburgh: Edinburgh University Press, 1974.

Lynch, Patricia. *Knights of God*. London: Bodley Head, 1967.

Maclean, Alistair. *Hebridean Altars*. Edinburgh: Moray, 1923.

Marsden, John. *Sea-Road of the Saints: Celtic Holy Men in the Hebrides*. Edinburgh: Floris Books, 1995.

Marshall, Peter. *Celtic Gold: A Voyage around Ireland*. London: Sinclair-Stevenson, 1997.

Matthews, Caitlin. *The Celtic Book of the Dead*. New York: St. Martin's, 1992. New edition: Atglen, PA: REDFeather (Schiffer), 2023.

Matthews, Caitlin. *A Celtic Devotional*. New Alresford, UK: Godsfield, 1997. New edition: East Lismore, New South Wales, Australia: Animal Dreaming, 2023.

Matthews, Caitlin. *Singing the Soul Back Home*. London: Eddison Books, 1968.

Matthews, John. *The Celtic Shaman*. Shaftsbury, UK: Element Books, 1995.

Matthews, John, and Caitlin Matthews. *The Encyclopaedia of Celtic Wisdom*. Shaftsbury, UK: Element Books, 1994.

Mayo, Margaret. *Saints, Birds & Beasts*. London: Kaye & Ward, 1980.

McNeill, John. *The Celtic Churches*. Chicago: University of Chicago Press, 1974.

Melia, Daniel. "The Irish Saint as Shaman." Pacific Coast Philology 18 (1983): 37–42.

Meyer, Kuno. *Ancient Irish Poetry*. London: Constable, 1913.

Nagy, Joseph Falaky. *Conversing with Angels & Ancients*. Dublin, Ireland: Four Courts, 1997.

O'Donoghue, John. *Anam Cara: Spiritual Wisdom from the Celtic World*. New York and London: Bantam, 1999.

O'Fiaich, Tomas. *Columbanus in His Own Words*. Dublin, Ireland: Veritas, 1974.

Palmer, James T. *Early Medieval Hagiography*. Leeds, UK: Arc Humanities Press, 2018.

Pennick, Nigel. *The Celtic Saints*. London: Thorsons/Godsfield,1997.

Ransome, Hilda. *The Sacred Bee in Ancient Times and Folklore*. New York: Dover Books, 2004.

Ryan, John. *Irish Monasticism*. Ithica, NY: Cornell University Press, 1972.

Sellner, Edward C. *Wisdom of the Celtic Saints*. Notre Dame, IN: Ave Maria, 1993.

Thomas, Patrick. *Candle in the Darkness: Celtic Spirituality from Wales*. Llandysul, Wales: Gomer, 1994.

Van der Weyer, Robert. *Celtic Fire*. New York, London: Doubleday, 1991.